THE ANIMAL ATLAS

Illustrated by Kenneth Lilly
Written by Barbara Taylor

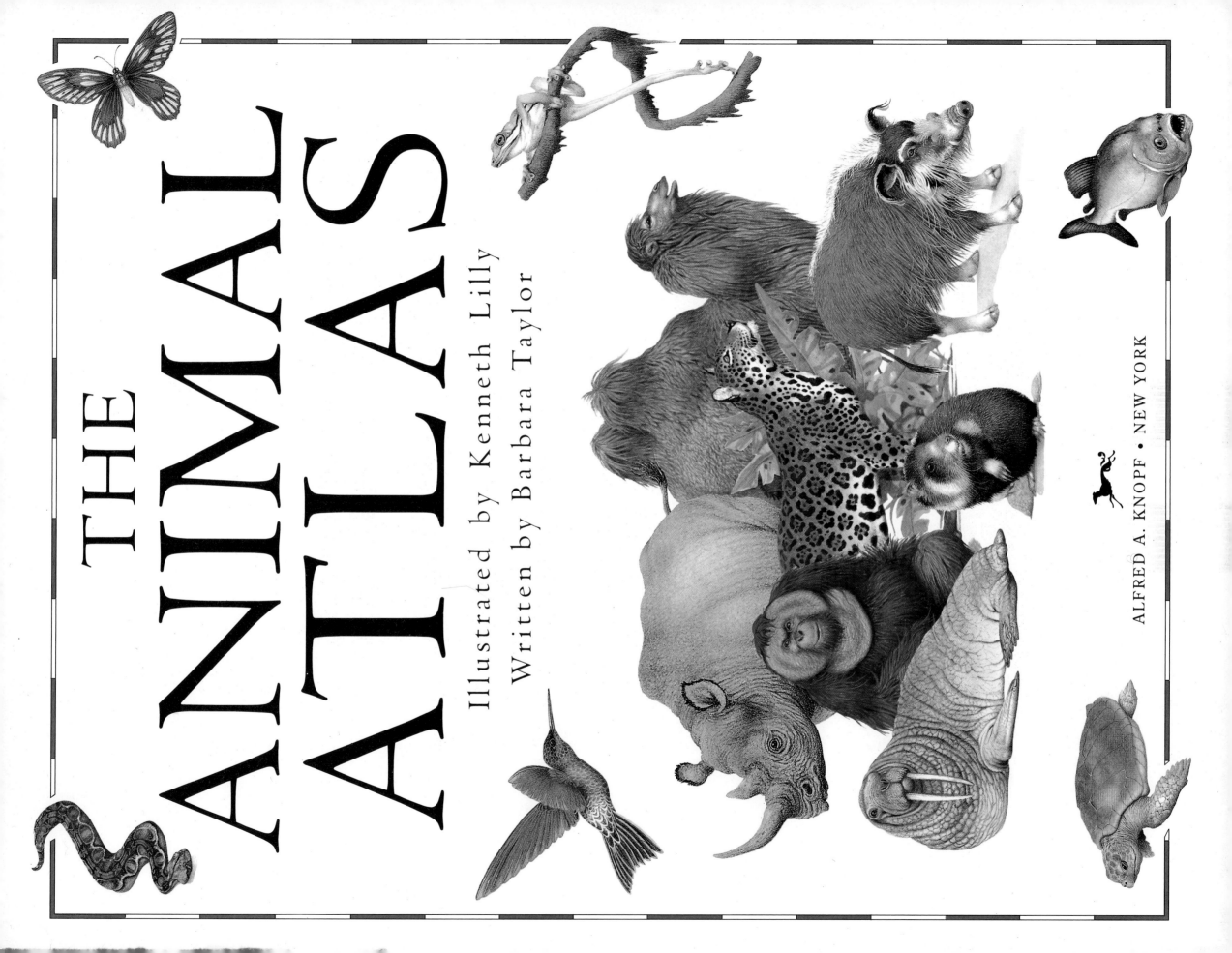

ALFRED A. KNOPF · NEW YORK

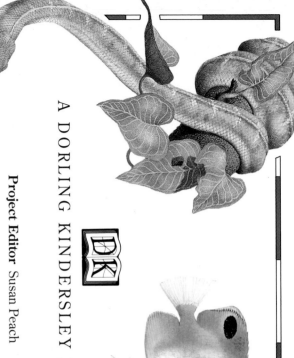

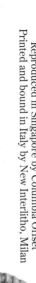

A DORLING KINDERSLEY BOOK

DK

Project Editor Susan Peach
Art Editor Richard Czapnik
Designer Marcus James
Production Teresa Solomon
Managing Editor Ann Kramer
Art Director Roger Priddy

Consultants Michael Chinery MA
and Keith Lye BA, FRGS

This is a Borzoi Book
published by Alfred A. Knopf, Inc.

First American edition, 1992

Copyright © 1992 Dorling Kindersley Limited, London. All rights
reserved under International and Pan-American Copyright Conventions.
Published in the United States by Alfred A. Knopf, Inc., New York.
Distributed by Random House, Inc., New York.
Published in Great Britain by Dorling Kindersley Limited, London.

Library of Congress Cataloging in Publication Data
Taylor, Barbara.
The animal atlas / written by Barbara Taylor;
illustrated by Kenneth Lilly.
p.   cm.
Includes index.
Summary: Depicts different habitats and the animals that live
there, including the Rocky Mountains, Amazon, European
woodlands, and Himalayas.
1. Animals – Pictorial works – Juvenile literature.
2. Animals – Habitat – Pictorial works – Juvenile literature.
[1. Animals – Habitat.] I. Title.
QL49.L65   1992   591.9 – dc20   91-53142
ISBN 0-679-80501-X
ISBN 0-679-90501-4 (lib. bdg.)

Reproduced in Singapore by Columbia Offset
Printed and bound in Italy by New Interlitho, Milan

CONTENTS

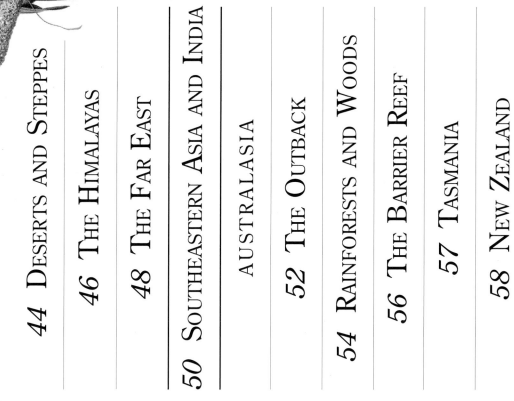

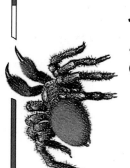

How to use this atlas

EACH DOUBLE-PAGE SPREAD in this atlas is about a particular habitat – the type of place where an animal lives. For example, the spread shown below is about European conifer forests. These habitats are arranged by continent, and there is a section in the book for each of the continents – North America, South America, Europe, Africa, Asia, Australasia, and Antarctica. The heading at the top of each page tells you which section you are in. Below you will learn what the maps and symbols on each spread show, and what the abbreviations stand for.

Where on Earth?
This globe shows you where in the world the habitat featured on the spread is situated and its rough extent. The red area on this globe, for example, shows the area covered by the European conifer forests.

Scale
You can use this scale to work out the size of the area shown on the map. The maps in the book have been drawn to different scales.

Direction
On the Arctic map, south is in all directions on the page; on the Antarctic, north. On all other maps, north is at the top of the page; south, at the bottom; east, to the right; west, to the left.

Latin names
Scientists have given each species of animal a Latin name so that people all over the world can use the same name no matter what language they speak. An animal's Latin name is divided into two parts. The first part is a group name given to a number of similar animals. For example, the group name for all the small cats is *Felis*. The second part of the name identifies the particular species of animal and often describes one of its specific characteristics. The full name for the wild cat shown here is *Felis sylvestris*, which means "cat of the woods."

Wild cat
(*Felis sylvestris*)

How big?
These labels give each animal's vital statistics – its height, length, or wingspan. Like people, animals of the same species vary in size, so the measurement given can only be approximate. Individual animals may be bigger or smaller than this size.

Length: 2 in

Animal symbols
The animal symbols on the map show the main animals featured on the spread. There is one symbol for each of the animals illustrated on the spread.

Map
The map shows the area and surrounding regions of the habitat featured on the spread. On this spread, for example, the map shows a large part of Europe, covering the conifer forests and the areas around them. You can see the shape and position of forests themselves on the top left-hand corner of the page. The main map shows major geographic features in the region, and where the animals live.

Scale
The animal symbols on the map show the main area where the animals can be found, but some animals are widely distributed over the whole region. There is one symbol for each of the animals illustrated on the spread.

Photos
The photographs around the map show you what the habitat looks like and what sort of vegetation can be found there.

Animal groups

MORE THAN A MILLION different kinds of animal have been discovered so far, but there are probably three or four times as many that people have never studied or named. Animals have several features in common. They move, breathe, feed, grow, have young, and respond rapidly to changes in their surroundings. To make animals easier to study, biologists divide them into a number of groups. The main groups are shown below.

Fish

Fish were the first group of vertebrates to evolve from invertebrates about 500 million years ago. There are about 22,000 species of fish alive today – more than all the mammals, birds, reptiles, and amphibians put together. Examples include butterfly fish and sharks.

Characteristics of fish:
• adapted to live in water
• absorb oxygen from the water through gills; a few have lungs as well
• swim by using fins
• bodies are covered with scales

Blue shark

Butterfly fish

Fish have fins in place of limbs. They use their fins to push and steer their way through the water.

Reptiles

Reptiles evolved from amphibians about 300 million years ago. About 6,100 species are alive today, including lizards, snakes, turtles and tortoises, and crocodiles. The dinosaurs were also reptiles.

Characteristics of reptiles:
• cannot maintain a constant body temperature; may sleep through very hot or very cold weather
• have dry, scaly skin, sometimes with bony plates for protection
• most live and breed on land
• breathe with lungs

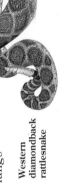

Western diamondback rattlesnake

Collared lizard

Turtles live in the sea but the female has to come ashore to lay her eggs, often on a sandy beach.

Mammals

Mammals evolved from reptiles about 200 million years ago, during the Age of the Dinosaurs. There are more than 4,000 species alive today, including kangaroos, rats, cats, dogs, elephants, whales, bats, deer, monkeys, and people.

Characteristics of mammals:
• mother feeds her young on milk
• bodies are covered with fur or hair
• can maintain a constant body temperature and have sweat glands to cool their bodies
• intelligent, with large brains
• breathe with lungs

Kangaroo rat

Siberian tiger

Female mammals suckle their young on milk produced in special mammary glands on their bodies.

Invertebrates

Invertebrates (animals without backbones) were the first animals to evolve on Earth, between 600 million and 1 billion years ago. Hundreds of thousands of species are alive today, and they far out number the vertebrates (animals with backbones). Invertebrates come in many different shapes and sizes, including microscopic moss-like animals, corals, jellyfish, insects, snails, spiders, crabs, centipedes, and worms.

Characteristic of invertebrates:
• do not have a backbone

Desert tarantula

Monarch butterfly

The starfish is an invertebrate that lives in water. It belongs to a group called echinoderms, which means "spiky skins."

Amphibians

Amphibians evolved from fishes over 350 million years ago. There are about 3,000 species alive today, including frogs, toads, newts, and salamanders.

Characteristics of amphibians:
• adults live mainly on land, but breed in water
• cannot maintain a constant body temperature
• skin is usually soft with no scales
• life cycle is usually in three stages – egg, larva (or tadpole), and adult
• adults breathe through lungs; tadpoles breathe through gills at first

Green toad

Japanese giant salamander

Tadpoles live in water for about 15 weeks while they develop into tiny frogs. They feed mainly on plants and small water creatures.

Birds

Birds evolved from reptiles about 140 million years ago. There are about 9,000 species alive today, including parrots, penguins, owls, songbirds, eagles, kiwis, and storks. Most birds can fly. They are adapted for flight by having wings instead of front legs, a light skeleton with hollow bones, and a covering of feathers.

Characteristics of birds:
• birds are the only animals with feathers
• breathe with lungs
• can maintain a constant body temperature
• lay eggs with hard, waterproof shells; usually incubate eggs with the heat of their bodies

Scarlet macaw

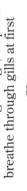

Kiwi

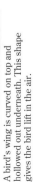

A bird's wing is curved on top and hollowed out underneath. This shape gives the bird lift in the air.

Animal habitats

ANIMALS LIVE ALL OVER THE WORLD, from the frozen Arctic wastes to the baking deserts. The type of place where an animal lives is called its habitat. Many species can live together in the same habitat because they eat different kinds of food or make their homes in different places. The animal life in any habitat is a finely balanced mixture of species, and the balance can be easily upset.

The map on these two pages shows the main types of habitat around the world. Animals have adapted to living in each of these habitats by developing characteristics that help them to survive. Similar types of habitat are found in different parts of the world, and the animals that live in them have developed similar adaptations. For instance, the kit fox that lives in the North American deserts looks very much like the fennec fox that lives in the Sahara Desert.

Physical barriers, such as mountains and seas, prevent many animals from moving freely from one place to another. Some animals can fly or swim across these barriers, so they spread over large areas. Storks, for example, fly across three continents, and tortoises can swim or float great distances across the sea.

Polar ice and tundra

The low temperatures, biting winds, and long, dark winters make the Arctic and Antarctic harsh environments for animals. Yet many animals do survive them, especially in the seas or on the frozen terrain around the Arctic, called the tundra. In the brief summer period, many animals migrate to the Arctic to breed and raise their young.

Find out more: pages 8–9, 42–43, 59.

Coniferous forests

The largest forests in the world stretch across the top of North America, Europe, and Asia. They are called the taiga. The trees are mostly conifers, such as fir and spruce, with needle-like leaves that stay on the trees all year round. These forests provide food and shelter for many animals, especially during the cold winter months.

Find out more: pages 10–11, 28–29, 42–43.

Deciduous woodlands

Deciduous woodlands are found south of the conifer forests, where the climate is mild and rainfall is plentiful throughout the year. The trees are mostly broadleaved species, such as oak and beech. They drop their leaves in the autumn and rest over the cooler winter months.

Find out more: pages 10–11, 30–31.

Grasslands

Grasslands grow in places where it is too dry for large areas of trees. The roots of the grasses bind the soil together, and the tops provide food for huge herds of grazing animals. Africa has tropical grasslands, called the savanna. North American prairies, South American pampas, and Asian steppes are cooler grasslands.

Find out more: pages 10–11, 26–27, 38–39, 44–45.

Scrubland

Dusty, dry land dotted with tough shrubs and small trees is found around the Mediterranean Sea, in parts of Australia, and in California. Rainfall is seasonal, and animals that live in these regions are adapted for survival through the long, dry, hot summers.

Find out more: pages 32–33.

Deciduous woods once spread across large areas of North America and Europe, but many of them have now been cut down.

The Everglades in Florida is a vast marshland area, covered with sawgrass.

Small, scrubby bushes are among the plants that survive in the dry regions around the Mediterranean Sea.

The pampas is a huge area of grassland in South America. Much of it is now used by farmers for grazing cattle.

PACIFIC OCEAN

NORTH AMERICA

SOUTH AMERICA

ATLANTIC OCEAN

ANTARCTICA

Deserts

It seldom rains in the deserts, so the animals that live in them have to survive without drinking for long periods or get all the water they need from their food. They also have to cope with baking-hot days and ice-cold nights. Many animals come out only at dawn and dusk when it is cooler and more humid.

Find out more: pages 14–15, 34–35, 44–45, 52–53.

Rainforests

Rainforests grow near the equator, where the weather is warm and humid all year round. Most of the trees are evergreen with broad leaves. Rainforests are home to the richest variety of wildlife to be found anywhere on Earth. More than 50 percent of all the different kinds of plants and animals in the world live in the rainforests.

Find out more: pages 24–25, 36–37, 54–55.

Marshland and swamp

Marshy, waterlogged places develop near lakes and rivers and along coasts. One of the largest marshland areas is the Everglades in Florida. Mangrove swamps often fringe the coasts in tropical areas. These two habitats are rich in food supplies and places to breed. They provide homes for a wide variety of animals, especially birds and insects.

Find out more: pages 16–17.

Mountains

Mountains are found in both warm and cold parts of the world. They provide a wide range of habitats for wildlife, from forest on the lower slopes to grassland and tundra farther up. The higher you go, the colder it becomes. Above a certain height – called the tree line – the temperature is too low for trees to survive. Even higher is the snow line. Above this it is so cold that the ground is always covered in snow and ice. The climate in mountainous regions can be severe, with low temperatures, fierce winds, and low rainfall. Mountain animals also have to cope with steep, slippery slopes.

Find out more: pages 12–13, 22–23, 46–47.

Coral reef

Coral reefs are made of the skeletons of tiny creatures called corals. Over millions of years they build up on top of one another to form a reef. Reefs develop only in warm, shallow, salty waters. A huge variety of fish, corals, sponges, and other animals live on a reef.

Find out more: page 56.

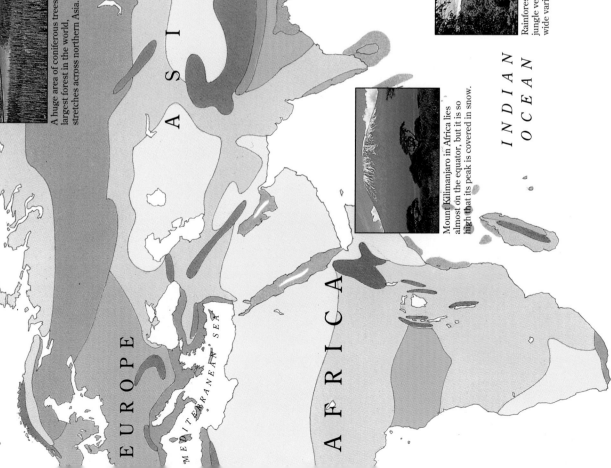

The biggest coral reef on Earth is the Great Barrier Reef, off the coast of northeastern Australia.

A huge area of coniferous trees, the largest forest in the world, stretches across northern Asia.

Rainforests are packed with dense jungle vegetation and are home to a wide variety of animals.

The central part of Australia – called the outback – consists of dry, rocky deserts where few plants can grow.

Mount Kilimanjaro in Africa lies almost on the equator, but it is so high that its peak is covered in snow.

Antarctica is the coldest and most isolated continent on Earth. Most of the land is covered by a thick ice cap.

EUROPE

ASIA

AFRICA

AUSTRALASIA

ANTARCTICA

MEDITERRANEAN SEA

INDIAN OCEAN

PACIFIC OCEAN

The Arctic

THE ARCTIC consists of the northernmost parts of North America, Europe, Asia, and a huge area of frozen ocean around the North Pole called the ice cap. It is one of the coldest places on Earth. The temperature rarely rises above 50°F, and in the winter it often drops to -40°F. There is a brief summer period when it is light for 24 hours a day. In the sea, light and warmth encourage the growth of tiny organisms called plankton, which are eaten by fishes, seals, and birds. On land, flowers bloom, providing food for millions of insects. Many birds, such as the Arctic tern and the brent goose, take advantage of this insect food supply by migrating to the Arctic to breed and raise their young. When the winter sets in again, these birds return to warmer climates. Some seals and whales also migrate south to warmer waters.

Lethal paws

The polar bear is a huge animal and can weigh as much as 10 adult people. It lives mainly on seals, often catching them at holes in the ice when they come up for air. One swipe from the bear's massive paw is enough to kill a seal. The bear then uses its claws to grab and hold on to its prey.

Polar bear
(*Ursus maritimus*)
Length: up to 8 ft 2 in
Height at shoulder: up to 5 ft 3 in

Longest hair

The musk ox has the longest coat of any mammal. Some hairs in its outer coat are more than 3 feet long. If a group of musk oxen are attacked, they form a tight circle facing outward and defend themselves with their sharp horns. The young stand in the middle of the circle for protection.

Musk ox
(*Ovibos moschatus*)
Length: 8 ft
Height at shoulder: up to 5 ft

Fearsome fly

The reindeer warble-fly lays its eggs in the fur of caribou and reindeer, which migrate to the Arctic in summer. When the eggs hatch, the grubs burrow through the skin and live in the deer's flesh. Eventually, the mature grubs drop to the ground and develop into adults.

Reindeer warble-fly
(*Oedemagena tarandi*)
Length: 0.5 in

Balloon nose

The male hooded seal has a strange balloon-like structure on the end of his nose. In the breeding season, he blows air into this structure until it is up to 12 inches long. The air in the "balloon" amplifies the loud calls that he makes to warn off other males. The hooded seal spends most of its life at sea, searching for fish and squid. It only comes out onto the ice to mate, breed, and molt, or shed its skin.

Hooded seal
(*Cystophora cristata*)
Length: up to 9 ft 9 in

Wonderful whiskers

The bearded seal lives in the seas around the edge of the ice cap. It has long, sensitive whiskers, which it uses to feel for shellfish on the seabed. It also feeds on fish and shrimp. In spring, the female hauls herself onto the ice to give birth.

Bearded seal
(*Erignathus barbatus*)
Length: up to 8 ft 2 in

Food store

During the summer the Arctic fox stores eggs, dead birds, and other food underneath rocks. Thanks to the cold climate, the food keeps as well as it would in a refrigerator. The fox eats it in the winter months, when fresh food is hard to find. The Arctic fox has a thick fur coat and can survive in temperatures as low as -58°F.

Arctic fox
(*Alopex lagopus*)
Body length: up to 2 ft 3 in
Tail: up to 16 in

Arctic unicorn

The narwhal is a small whale that stays in the Arctic. It has only two teeth. One of the male's teeth grows into a long, spiraling tusk that sticks out through a hole in his top lip. No one knows what this tusk is for, although males have been seen fighting one another with their tusks.

Narwhal
(*Monodon monoceros*)
Body length: up to 15 ft
Tusk: 9 ft 10 in

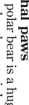

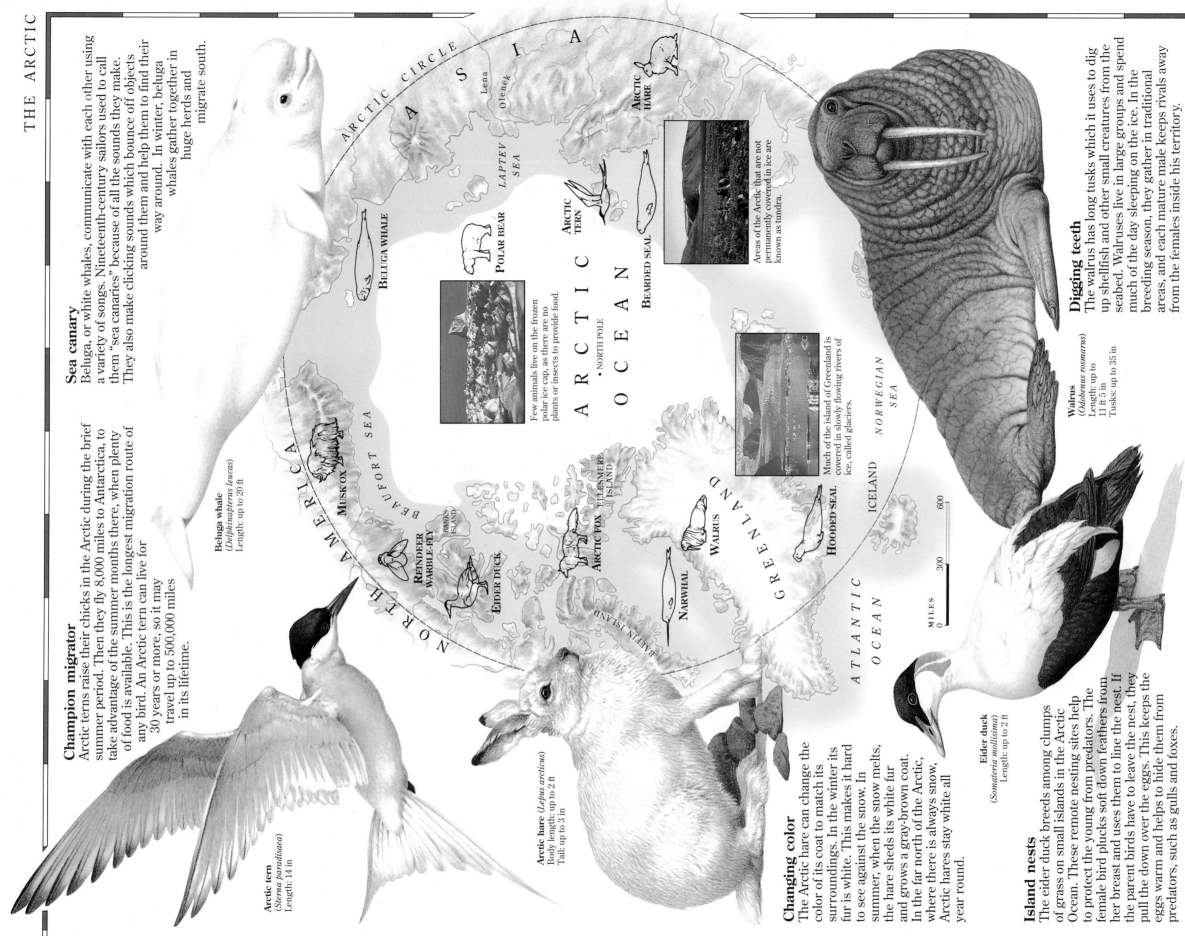

Champion migrator

Arctic terns raise their chicks in the Arctic during the brief summer period. Then they fly 8,000 miles to Antarctica, to take advantage of the summer months there, when plenty of food is available. This is the longest migration route of any bird. An Arctic tern can live for 30 years or more, so it may travel up to 500,000 miles in its lifetime.

Arctic tern
(*Sterna paradisaea*)
Length: 14 in

Sea canary

Beluga, or white whales, communicate with each other using a variety of songs. Nineteenth-century sailors used to call them "sea canaries" because of all the sounds they make. They also make clicking sounds which bounce off objects around them and help them to find their way around. In winter, beluga whales gather together in huge herds and migrate south.

Beluga whale
(*Delphinapterus leucas*)
Length: up to 20 ft

BELUGA WHALE

MUSK OX

REINDEER WARBLE-FLY

EIDER DUCK

POLAR BEAR

Few animals live on the frozen polar ice cap, as there are no plants or insects to provide food.

ARCTIC TERN

BEARDED SEAL

Areas of the Arctic that are not permanently covered in ice are known as tundra.

ARCTIC HARE

A S I A

Lena

Olenek

LAPTEV SEA

ARCTIC CIRCLE

A R C T I C   O C E A N

• NORTH POLE

NORWEGIAN SEA

ICELAND

Much of the island of Greenland is covered in slowly flowing rivers of ice, called glaciers.

G R E E N L A N D

ARCTIC FOX

NARWHAL

WALRUS

HOODED SEAL

N O R T H   A M E R I C A

BEAUFORT SEA

BANKS ISLAND

ELLESMERE ISLAND

BAFFIN ISLAND

A T L A N T I C   O C E A N

MILES
0   300   600

Changing color

The Arctic hare can change the color of its coat to match its surroundings. In the winter its fur is white. This makes it hard to see against the snow. In summer, when the snow melts, the hare sheds its white fur and grows a gray-brown coat. In the far north of the Arctic, where there is always snow, Arctic hares stay white all year round.

Arctic hare (*Lepus arcticus*)
Body length: up to 2 ft
Tail: up to 3 in

Island nests

The eider duck breeds among clumps of grass on small islands in the Arctic Ocean. These remote nesting sites help to protect the young from predators. The female bird plucks soft down feathers from her breast and uses them to line the nest. If the parent birds have to leave the nest, they pull the down over the eggs. This keeps the eggs warm and helps to hide them from predators, such as gulls and foxes.

Eider duck
(*Somateria mollisima*)
Length: up to 2 ft

Digging teeth

The walrus has long tusks which it uses to dig up shellfish and other small creatures from the seabed. Walruses live in large groups and spend much of the day sleeping on the ice. In the breeding season, they gather in traditional areas, and each mature male keeps rivals away from the females inside his territory.

Walrus
(*Odobenus rosmarus*)
Length: up to 11 ft 5 in
Tusks: up to 35 in

Forests, Lakes, and Prairies

THE EVERGREEN FORESTS OF CANADA consist of dense areas of spruce, pine, and fir trees. These forests are marshy underfoot and contain many lakes. Farther south are forests of oak and hickory trees. They once spread right across the eastern part of North America, but vast areas of these forests have been destroyed for timber or to clear land for farming. Some of the forest animals, such as the raccoon and the opossum, have adapted to the more open environment, but many animals have declined in numbers or retreated to the hills and mountains. The prairies once formed a huge sea of grass. Millions of bison and pronghorn antelope used to graze on the prairies, but in the 1800s they were almost wiped out by hunters. Both animals are now protected species. Today much of this region is used for farming.

Sage grouse
(*Centrocercus urophasianus*)
Length: up to 18 in

Flavored flesh
The sage grouse feeds on the leaves of the sagebrush plant and, in time, its flesh takes on the flavor of sage. In spring, the male puts on a special display to win a mate. He puffs out his chest feathers, opens and closes his tail, and inflates the air sacs on his neck. He also makes loud, booming calls.

Moose (*Alces alces*)
Height at shoulder:
up to 6 ft 6 in
Length: up to 10 ft

Two-spotted ladybug
(*Adalia bipunctata*)
Length: 0.25 in

Big cheeks
The least chipmunk has large cheek pouches in which it carries food back to its underground burrow. Inside the burrow are chambers used for living, nesting, and storing food. In winter, the chipmunk hibernates in the burrow.

Raccoon
(*Procyon lotor*)
Body length:
up to 2 ft 2 in
Tail: up to 12 in

Pest control
The two-spotted ladybug is common throughout North America. It lives in a range of habitats, including forests, fields, and gardens. It feeds on small insects and is valued for keeping down the number of pests in gardens and fields. The ladybug's hard, red wing cases protect its wings and delicate body.

Heavyweight deer
The moose is the largest deer in the world. In the fall, a male may weigh more than 1,000 pounds. The moose has broad hooves and long legs, enabling it to travel through deep snow, bogs, or lakes. Its overhanging top lip helps it to tear off leaves and tender twigs. In the fall, the males compete for mates by fighting with their antlers.

Least chipmunk
(*Eutamias minimus*)
Body length: up to 4.5 in
Tail: up to 4.5 in

Garbage can raider
The raccoon has long, sensitive fingers with which it searches for food. It often comes into cities and raids garbage cans for food scraps. The raccoon's thick fur keeps it warm during the cold winter months.

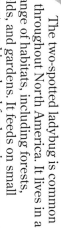

Whooping crane
(*Grus americana*)
Height: 5 ft
Wingspan: 7 ft 6 in

Bugle bird
The whooping crane is named after its buglelike, whooping call. It nests only in a remote area of northwest Canada. By the 1940s the whooping crane had been almost wiped out by hunting. It is now a protected species.

The forest lakes are home to many water birds, including gulls, ducks, and swans.

Yukon
BALD EAGLE
MOOSE

PACIFIC OCEAN

R O

Today most of the flat prairie lands are used for growing wheat.

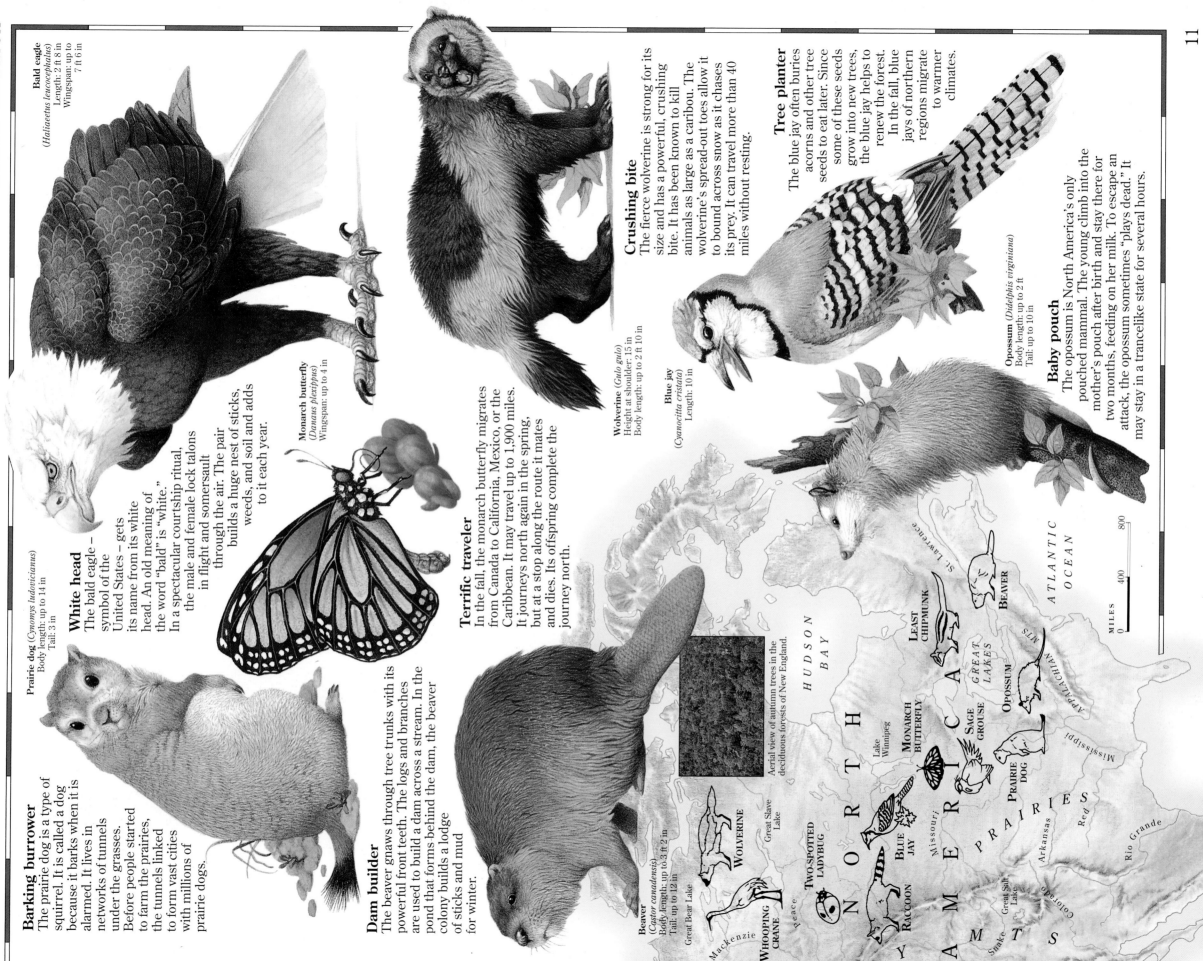

Bald eagle
(Haliaeetus leucocephalus)
Length: 2 ft 8 in
Wingspan: up to
7 ft 6 in

Barking burrower
The prairie dog is a type of squirrel. It is called a dog because it barks when it is alarmed. It lives in networks of tunnels under the grasses. Before people started to farm the prairies, the tunnels linked to form vast cities with millions of prairie dogs.

Prairie dog *(Cynomys ludovicianus)*
Body length: up to 14 in
Tail: 3 in

White head
The bald eagle – symbol of the United States – gets its name from its white head. An old meaning of the word "bald" is "white." In a spectacular courtship ritual, the male and female lock talons in flight and somersault through the air. The pair builds a huge nest of sticks, weeds, and soil and adds to it each year.

Monarch butterfly
(Danaus plexippus)
Wingspan: up to 4 in

Dam builder
The beaver gnaws through tree trunks with its powerful front teeth. The logs and branches are used to build a dam across a stream. In the pond that forms behind the dam, the beaver colony builds a lodge of sticks and mud for winter.

Beaver
(Castor canadensis)
Body length: up to 3 ft 2 in
Tail: up to 12 in

Terrific traveler
In the fall, the monarch butterfly migrates from Canada to California, Mexico, or the Caribbean. It may travel up to 1,900 miles. It journeys north again in the spring, but at a stop along the route it mates and dies. Its offspring complete the journey north.

Aerial view of autumn trees in the deciduous forests of New England.

Crushing bite
The fierce wolverine is strong for its size and has a powerful, crushing bite. It has been known to kill animals as large as a caribou. The wolverine's spread-out toes allow it to bound across snow as it chases its prey. It can travel more than 40 miles without resting.

Wolverine *(Gulo gulo)*
Height at shoulder: 15 in
Body length: up to 2 ft 10 in

Blue jay
(Cyanocitta cristata)
Length: 10 in

Tree planter
The blue jay often buries acorns and other tree seeds to eat later. Since some of these seeds grow into new trees, the blue jay helps to renew the forest. In the fall, blue jays of northern regions migrate to warmer climates.

Opossum *(Didelphis virginiana)*
Body length: up to 2 ft
Tail: up to 10 in

Baby pouch
The opossum is North America's only pouched mammal. The young climb into the mother's pouch after birth and stay there for two months, feeding on her milk. To escape an attack, the opossum sometimes "plays dead." It may stay in a trancelike state for several hours.

MILES
0   400   800

ATLANTIC OCEAN

HUDSON BAY

St. Lawrence

Mackenzie

Great Bear Lake

Great Slave Lake

Peace

Lake Winnipeg

WOLVERINE

WHOOPING CRANE

TWO-SPOTTED LADYBUG

MONARCH BUTTERFLY

BLUE JAY

RACCOON

SAGE GROUSE

LEAST CHIPMUNK

GREAT LAKES

BEAVER

OPOSSUM

APPALACHIAN MTS.

PRAIRIE DOG

Missouri

Red

Arkansas

Snake

Great Salt Lake

Colorado

Rio Grande

Mississippi

NORTH AMERICA

PRAIRIES

ROCKY MTS.

The Rockies

THE ROCKIES ARE A VAST range of mountains that stretch down the western side of North America. They form a barrier to the moist winds that sweep eastward from the Pacific Ocean. As these winds rise up over the mountains and cool, the water they carry falls as rain or snow. On the mountain peaks, winds can reach speeds of 200 mph and temperatures may fall to -60°F.

The Rockies provide a refuge for animals that have been hunted or driven out of other habitats by people. Some species are specially adapted for climbing and jumping on the mountain slopes. Many of the animals have warm fur to protect them against the cold and the winds. In winter, some animals shelter in the forests on the lower slopes.

Grizzled giant
The huge grizzly bear gets its name from its coarse, gray-tipped (grizzled), brown fur. A grizzly can kill an animal as large as a moose or caribou, but it usually feeds on smaller animals, fish, and plants. It catches fish with a swipe of its front paw. A grizzly can run as fast as a horse for short distances and may stand up on its back legs to get a better view. In the fall, the grizzly eats as much as possible. It builds up stores of fat that last through its winter hibernation.

Grizzly bear
(*Ursus arctos horribilis*)
Height standing on back legs: up to 10 ft

Snowshoe hare
(*Lepus americanus*)
Length: up to 20 in

Spotted camouflage
The bobcat's spotted coat blends in with a rocky or forested background, enabling the animal to creep up on its prey without being seen. The bobcat usually hunts rabbits and hares but will eat almost any reptile, mammal, or bird. It can even kill a deer, which provides enough food for a week or more.

Bobcat (*Lynx rufus*)
Height at shoulder: 22 in
Length: up to 3 ft 3 in

Winter white
In summer the snowshoe hare has brown fur. In winter it grows a white coat that matches the snowy ground. It also grows dense fur on its feet, making them look like snowshoes. The fur keeps the hare's feet warm and stops the animal from sinking into the snow.

Bighorn sheep (*Ovis canadensis*)
Body length: up to 6 ft
Horns: up to 3 ft

Nonskid feet
The bighorn sheep is good at climbing and jumping on the steep mountain slopes. Its two-toed hooves separate on uneven ground, which helps the sheep grip the rocks. The male has curving horns, which he uses to fight rival males.

Porcupine
(*Erethizon dorsatum*)
Body length: up to 2 ft 6 in
Tail: up to 11 in

Spiky armor
The porcupine's stiff fur hides about 30,000 sharp quills. If threatened, the porcupine turns its back, raises its quills, and lashes its tail. The tail quills are barbed like arrows and get stuck in the skin of the attacker.

Summer butterfly
Male phoebus butterflies appear in the Rockies in mid-summer, eight to ten days before the females. They mate soon after the female emerges from her cocoon, often before she is able to fly.

Phoebus butterfly
(*Parnassius phoebus*)
Wingspan: up to 3.5 in

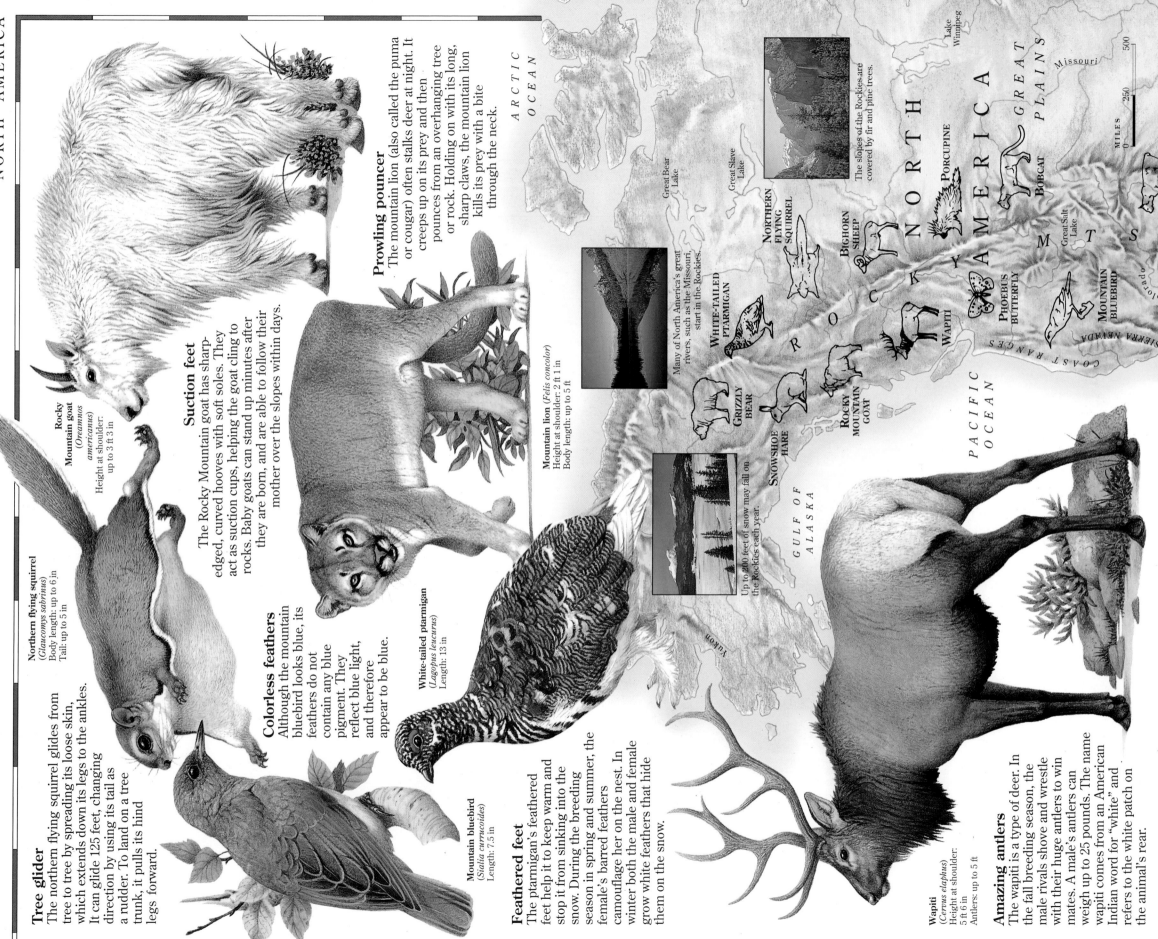

Tree glider
The northern flying squirrel glides from tree to tree by spreading its loose skin, which extends down its legs to the ankles. It can glide 125 feet, changing direction by using its tail as a rudder. To land on a tree trunk, it pulls its hind legs forward.

Northern flying squirrel
(*Glaucomys sabrinus*)
Body length: up to 6 in
Tail: up to 5 in

Rocky Mountain goat
(*Oreamnos americanus*)
Height at shoulder: up to 3 ft 3 in

Suction feet
The Rocky Mountain goat has sharp-edged, curved hooves with soft soles. They act as suction cups, helping the goat cling to rocks. Baby goats can stand up minutes after they are born, and are able to follow their mother over the slopes within days.

Colorless feathers
Although the mountain bluebird looks blue, its feathers do not contain any blue pigment. They reflect blue light, and therefore appear to be blue.

Mountain bluebird
(*Sialia currucoides*)
Length: 7.5 in

Feathered feet
The ptarmigan's feathered feet help it to keep warm and stop it from sinking into the snow. During the breeding season in spring and summer, the female's barred feathers camouflage her on the nest. In winter both the male and female grow white feathers that hide them on the snow.

White-tailed ptarmigan
(*Lagopus leucurus*)
Length: 13 in

Prowling pouncer
The mountain lion (also called the puma or cougar) often stalks deer at night. It creeps up on its prey and then pounces from an overhanging tree or rock. Holding on with its long, sharp claws, the mountain lion kills its prey with a bite through the neck.

Mountain lion (*Felis concolor*)
Height at shoulder: 2 ft 1 in
Body length: up to 5 ft

Amazing antlers
The wapiti is a type of deer. In the fall breeding season, the male rivals shove and wrestle with their huge antlers to win mates. A male's antlers can weigh up to 25 pounds. The name wapiti comes from an American Indian word for "white" and refers to the white patch on the animal's rear.

Wapiti
(*Cervus elaphus*)
Height at shoulder: 5 ft 6 in
Antlers: up to 5 ft

ARCTIC OCEAN

NORTH AMERICA

ROCKY MOUNTAINS

GREAT PLAINS

The slopes of the Rockies are covered by fir and pine trees.

Lake Winnipeg

Missouri

MILES
0   250   500

Great Bear Lake

Great Slave Lake

Great Salt Lake

NORTHERN FLYING SQUIRREL

BIGHORN SHEEP

PORCUPINE

BOBCAT

MOUNTAIN LION

PHOEBUS BUTTERFLY

WAPITI

MOUNTAIN BLUEBIRD

SIERRA NEVADA

COAST RANGES

WHITE-TAILED PTARMIGAN

Many of North America's great rivers, such as the Missouri, start in the Rockies.

GRIZZLY BEAR

ROCKY MOUNTAIN GOAT

SNOWSHOE HARE

GULF OF ALASKA

PACIFIC OCEAN

Colorado

Yukon

Up to 200 feet of snow may fall on the Rockies each year.

Western Deserts

THE STONY DESERTS OF NORTH AMERICA cover large areas of the southwestern United States and northern Mexico. The largest of the deserts is the Great Basin, which is sandwiched between two ranges of mountains – the Rockies to the east and the Sierras to the west. To the south, the Great Basin merges with the Mojave Desert. Between the two lies Death Valley, one of the hottest places on Earth. South of the Mojave is the Sonoran Desert, which is famous for its giant saguaro cacti.

The desert is a harsh environment, but many animals survive there, making the most of what little moisture is available. Some animals are adapted to survive without drinking at all. Many animals stay in burrows during the day, emerging only at night when the air is cooler and damper.

Antenna ears

The kit fox is the smallest fox in North America. It comes out at night to hunt, using its huge ears as antennae to track down its prey. The kit fox eats small animals, such as lizards, and is able to run very swiftly to overtake and seize them before they disappear down their burrows.

Kit fox (*Vulpes macrotis*)
Body length: up to 11 in
Tail: up to 22 in

Spiny fortress

The cactus wren builds a large, domed nest among the spines of a cactus or a thorny bush, where its young are well protected from predators. The bird's tough feathers and hard, scaly legs protect it from scratches. The wren may keep old nests in repair to serve as roosts during the winter.

Cactus wren
(*Campylorhynchus brunneicapillus*)
Length: up to 8.5 in

Smelly defense

The spotted skunk protects itself from predators by spraying them with an evil-smelling liquid that comes from scent glands under its tail. The skunk often aims for the eyes, and it can hit a target accurately from 12 feet away. Before it sprays, the skunk does a handstand, displaying its striking black and white fur. This is a warning that the skunk will spray if it isn't left alone. The skunk comes out mainly at night to hunt for small animals, eggs, insects, and fruit.

Spotted skunk (*Spilogale putorius*)
Body length: up to 14 in
Tail: up to 9 in

Speedy bird

The roadrunner lives on the ground and rarely flies. It has extremely powerful legs and can run at speeds of up to 15 miles per hour. Its long tail acts as a brake or rudder, allowing the bird to swerve suddenly or come to an abrupt halt. The roadrunner is very strong and can kill a snake by stabbing with its sharp beak.

Roadrunner
(*Geococcyx californianus*)
Body length: up to 2 ft
Tail: 12 in

Warning rattle

The western diamondback rattlesnake has a "rattle" on its tail, which it shakes to scare away animals that might tread on it. The rattle is made up of loose rings of hard skin. One of these rings is left behind each time the snake sheds its skin. Rattlesnakes are poisonous and kill small animals by striking them with their long fangs.

Western diamondback rattlesnake
(*Crotalus atrox*) Length: up to 7 ft

Trailing tails

The desert swallowtail butterfly is named after the long, trailing tails on its back wings, which resemble a swallow's tail. It lives in the mountain canyons of the desert and only breeds after it rains. The caterpillars of this butterfly give off a foul odor if they are disturbed. This helps to discourage predators.

Desert swallowtail
(*Papilio coloro*)
Wingspan: up to 3 in

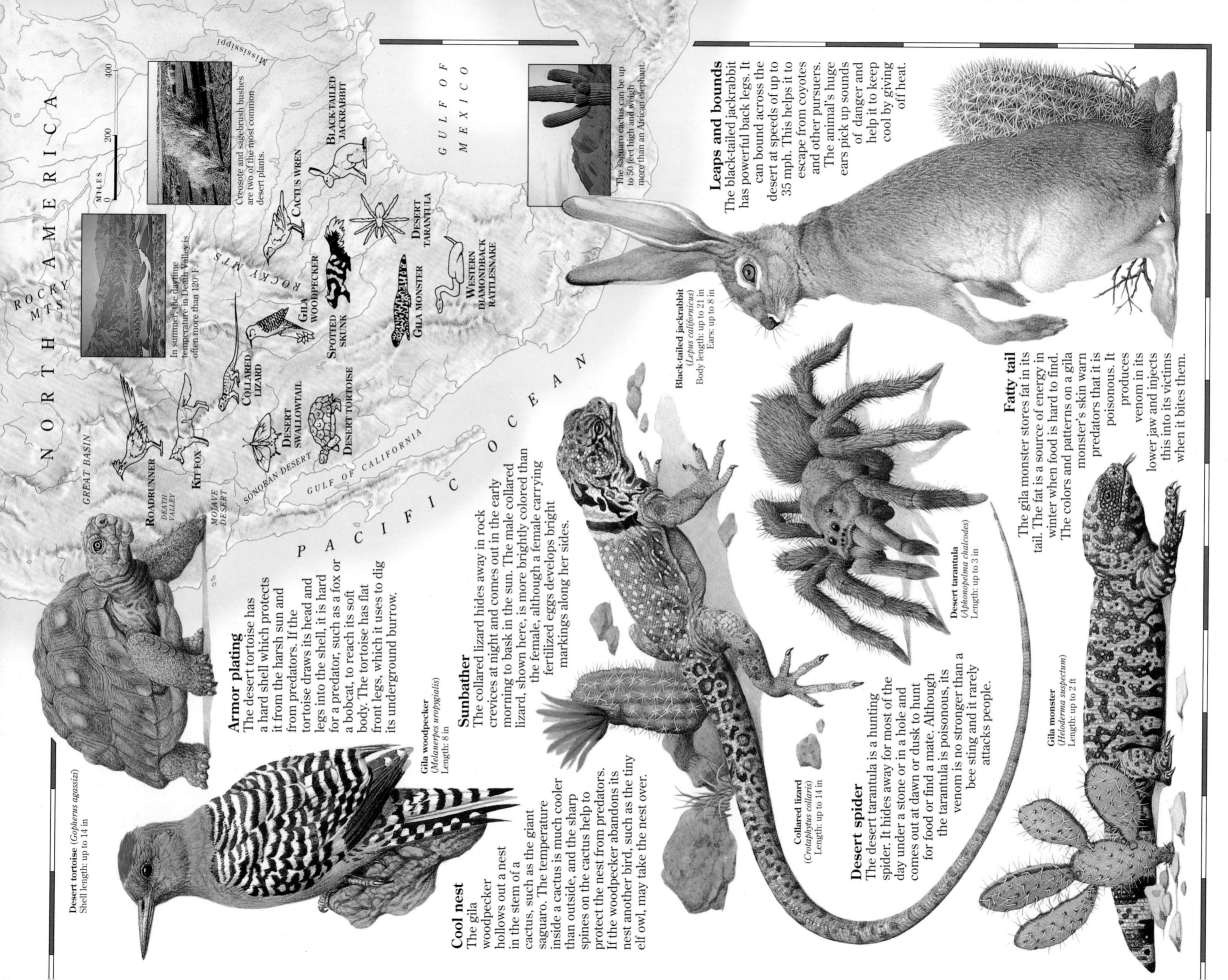

NORTH AMERICA

ROCKY MTS

GREAT BASIN

Mississippi

MILES
0   200   400

Creosote and sagebrush bushes are two of the most common desert plants.

In summer, the daytime temperature in Death Valley is often more than 120°F.

ROCKY MTS

CACTUS WREN

BLACK-TAILED JACKRABBIT

GILA WOODPECKER

DESERT TARANTULA

SPOTTED SKUNK

WESTERN DIAMONDBACK RATTLESNAKE

COLLARED LIZARD

GILA MONSTER

DESERT TORTOISE

DESERT SWALLOWTAIL

KIT FOX

ROADRUNNER

DEATH VALLEY

MOJAVE DESERT

SONORAN DESERT

GULF OF CALIFORNIA

GULF OF MEXICO

PACIFIC OCEAN

The Saguaro cactus can be up to 50 feet high and weigh more than an African elephant.

Leaps and bounds
The black-tailed jackrabbit has powerful back legs. It can bound across the desert at speeds of up to 35 mph. This helps it to escape from coyotes and other pursuers. The animal's huge ears pick up sounds of danger and help it to keep cool by giving off heat.

Black-tailed jackrabbit
(*Lepus californicus*)
Body length: up to 21 in
Ears: up to 8 in

Armor plating
The desert tortoise has a hard shell which protects it from the harsh sun and from predators. If the tortoise draws its head and legs into the shell, it is hard for a predator, such as a fox or a bobcat, to reach its soft body. The tortoise has flat front legs, which it uses to dig its underground burrow.

Desert tortoise (*Gopherus agassizi*)
Shell length: up to 14 in

Cool nest
The gila woodpecker hollows out a nest in the stem of a cactus, such as the giant saguaro. The temperature inside a cactus is much cooler than outside, and the sharp spines on the cactus help to protect the nest from predators. If the woodpecker abandons its nest another bird, such as the tiny elf owl, may take the nest over.

Gila woodpecker
(*Melanerpes uropygialis*)
Length: 8 in

Sunbather
The collared lizard hides away in rock crevices at night and comes out in the early morning to bask in the sun. The male collared lizard, shown here, is more brightly colored than the female, although a female carrying fertilized eggs develops bright markings along her sides.

Collared lizard
(*Crotaphytus collaris*)
Length: up to 14 in

Desert spider
The desert tarantula is a hunting spider. It hides away for most of the day under a stone or in a hole and comes out at dawn or dusk to hunt for food or find a mate. Although the tarantula is poisonous, its venom is no stronger than a bee sting and it rarely attacks people.

Desert tarantula
(*Aphonopelma chalcodes*)
Length: up to 3 in

Fatty tail
The gila monster stores fat in its tail. The fat is a source of energy in winter when food is hard to find. The colors and patterns on a gila monster's skin warn predators that it is poisonous. It produces venom in its lower jaw and injects this into its victims when it bites them.

Gila monster
(*Heloderma suspectum*)
Length: up to 2 ft

The Everglades

THE SEMI-TROPICAL MARSHLAND of the Everglades National Park covers an area of 2,120 square miles in southern Florida. The Everglades is an enormous swamp with grass covering most of the swamp, broken only by islands of trees. There are two main seasons in the Everglades: the wet summer and the dry winter. In the summer, the higher water levels allow the animals to move freely throughout the park. But in winter they gather around the few remaining water holes.

The park provides a rich feeding and breeding ground for large numbers of insects, fish, reptiles, and birds. Many rare animals, such as the Florida panther and the manatee, live there. Unfortunately, pesticides and fertilizers used on neighboring farms are polluting the water, and the Everglades is also threatened by drainage schemes to the north of the park.

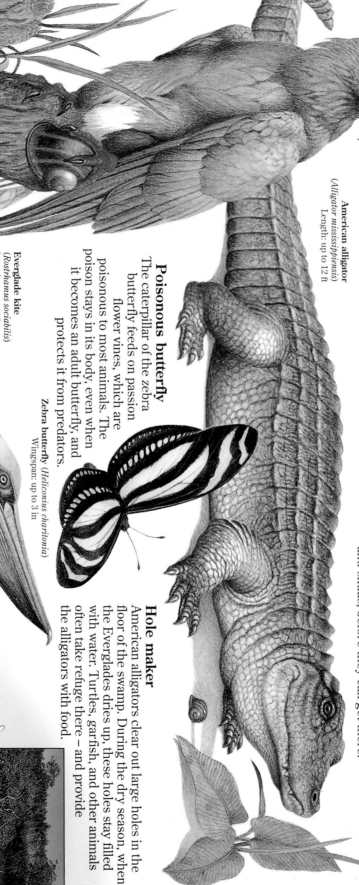

American alligator
(*Alligator mississippiensis*)
Length: up to 12 ft

Everglade kite
(*Rostrhamus sociabilis*)
Length: up to 18 in
Wingspan: 3 ft 8 in

Snail diet
The Everglade kite is also called the snail kite because it eats only one type of water snail, called *Pomacea*. The kite uses its slender, hooked beak to pry out the snail's soft body without breaking its shell. Everglade kites nest in huge colonies and search for food in groups.

Brown pelican
(*Pelecanus occidentalis*)
Length: up to 4 ft 6 in
Wingspan: 8 ft 2 in

Poisonous butterfly
The caterpillar of the zebra butterfly feeds on passion flower vines, which are poisonous to most animals. The poison stays in its body, even when it becomes an adult butterfly, and protects it from predators.

Zebra butterfly (*Heliconius charitonia*)
Wingspan: up to 3 in

Super diver
The brown pelican feeds on fish. To catch its prey, it makes a spectacular dive into the sea and scoops up a fish and a mouthful of water in the huge pouch under its beak. Often this water weighs twice as much as the bird itself. A brown pelican can scoop up a fish in less than two seconds.

Heat sensors
The cottonmouth snake, or water moccasin, hunts at night. Like all pit vipers, it has two small holes, called pits, on its face. The snake can sense heat with these pits, so it can find the warm bodies of small animals and birds in the dark. The cottonmouth kills its prey with its poisonous fangs.

Cottonmouth
(*Agkistrodon piscivorus*)
Length: up to 6 ft

Hole maker
American alligators clear out large holes in the floor of the Everglades swamp. During the dry season, when the Everglades dries up, these holes stay filled with water. Turtles, garfish, and other animals often take refuge there – and provide the alligators with food.

Islands of trees, called hammocks, stick up above the water level.

Dangerous journey
The female loggerhead turtle comes ashore at night to lay her eggs on the beach. She digs a hole, lays more than a hundred eggs, covers them with sand, and then heads back to sea. After about eight weeks, the baby turtles hatch out and make their way as quickly as they can to the safety of the sea. Many of them are eaten by seabirds, such as gulls and skuas, before they can get there.

Loggerhead turtle
(*Caretta caretta*)
Length: up to 4 ft

Sticky toes

The green tree frog has sticky suction pads on its toes which enable it to grip smooth, slippery surfaces. Most adult tree frogs can change their color or pattern in response to temperature, light, or moisture, although this may take an hour or more. The tree frog is so small and light that a leaf can take its weight.

Green tree frog (*Hyla cinerea*)
Length: up to 2.5 in

Power jaws

The garpike looks like a drifting log as it lurks among the reeds. But it has powerful jaws and fearsome teeth, and it can snatch fish and other animals from the water with a sideways slash of its snout. The garpike has gills for breathing underwater, but it can also breathe air if the water dries up. The garpike is an ancient species. Its ancestors were alive 150 million years ago in the days of the dinosaurs, and the fish has hardly changed since.

Garpike (*Lepisosteus osseus*)
Length: up to 8 ft

Manatee (*Trichechus manatus*)
Length: up to 12 ft 6 in

Speedy swimmer

The manatee is a rare mammal that lives entirely in the water. It is a good swimmer, using its flattened tail to push itself through the water at speeds of 15 mph or more. The manatee can stay underwater for up to 15 minutes, but it has to come to the surface to breathe air. It can weigh nearly 2,200 pounds and needs to eat 65 pounds of plant food a day to stay alive.

Roseate spoonbill (*Ajaia ajaja*)
Length: up to 2 ft 8 in
Wingspan: 4 ft 3 in

Spoon feeding

The roseate spoonbill is named after its spoon-shaped bill, which it uses to feel for food in the muddy water of the Everglades. The bird feeds on small fishes, shrimp, and shellfish. It sweeps its partly open bill from side to side and snaps it shut when it touches its prey.

BISCAYNE BAY

ATLANTIC OCEAN

Mangroves are among the most common Everglade trees. They can grow to a height of 80 feet.

F L O R I D A

MILES
0   6   12

The Seminole Indians called the Everglades area "Pa-hay-okee," which means "river of grass."

BOUNDARY OF EVERGLADES NATIONAL PARK

COTTONMOUTH

PAINTED BUNTING

AMERICAN ALLIGATOR

GARPIKE

EVERGLADE KITE

ZEBRA BUTTERFLY

GREEN TREE FROG

BROWN PELICAN

ROSEATE SPOONBILL

MANATEE

Broad

Harney

Shark

LOGGERHEAD TURTLE

MOSQUITO

FLORIDA BAY

K E Y S

F L O R I D A

GULF OF MEXICO

Mosquito
(*Aedes species*)
Length: up to 0.2 in

Blood meal

The female mosquito needs a meal of blood before she can lay eggs. She bites a mammal and sucks its blood, then lays her eggs in a pool. The larvae develop underwater and have a breathing tube on the end of the abdomen so they can take in air from above the surface of the water.

Painted bunting
(*Passerina ciris*)
Length: up to 5.5 in

Attractive colors

The male painted bunting is the only bird with a blue head and bright red underparts. His beautiful colors help him to attract a mate. The female is all green, which provides camouflage while she is sitting on the nest. Painted buntings have strong beaks which they use to crush seeds and remove the husks.

Central America

THE VARIED WILDLIFE of Central America and the islands of the Caribbean Sea reflects the many different habitats in the region.

These habitats range from mangrove swamps on the coasts to grassland and rainforest inland. The climate in the region is warm all year round, but there are violent storms and hurricanes in the summer and autumn.

Central America forms an important land bridge along which animals can pass between North and South America. Although the Caribbean islands are close to Central America, the sea has prevented many animals from reaching them. Several unusual animals, such as the solenodon, have evolved on the islands, where they have few enemies or competitors.

Blood sucker
The vampire bat preys on large mammals, such as cattle. It has razor-sharp front teeth which it uses to puncture its victim's skin. It then laps up the blood that oozes from the wound. The bat does not take enough blood to kill its victims, but its saliva can pass on rabies and other diseases.

Vampire bat
(*Desmodus rotundus*)
Length: up to 3.5 in
Wingspan: up to 7 in

Smallest bird
The tiny bee hummingbird, which lives in Cuba, is the smallest bird in the world. It beats its wings faster than the human eye can see, at 30–80 beats per second, producing a humming sound like a bee. It sips nectar from flowers and must feed very often because it uses so much energy to fly.

Bee hummingbird
(*Mellisuga helenae*)
Length: 2 in

Deadly snake
The fer-de-lance is one of the most aggressive snakes on Earth – it is quick to strike and very poisonous. The fer-de-lance injects its prey with a paralyzing venom. The patterns on the snake's skin blend into the leaf litter on the forest floor. This makes the snake almost impossible to spot.

Fer-de-lance snake
(*Bothrops atrox*)
Length: up to 6 ft 6 in

Trap jaws
The trap-jaw ant has huge jaws, which it uses for hunting and for carrying things. The ant in the picture is carrying a pupa, which is changing into an adult ant inside its case.

Trap-jaw ant
(*Acanthognathus teledectes*)
Length: 0.1 in

See-through frog
The glass frog gets its name because the skin on its belly is transparent. The frog lives in the rainforest and lays its eggs on the leaves of a plant overhanging a stream. One of the parents, usually the male, guards the eggs until they hatch. The tadpoles fall out of the eggs into the water below, where they develop into adult frogs.

Glass frog
(*Centrolenella vireovittata*)
Length: up to 1 in

Aerial acrobat
The kinkajou spends most of its life swinging like an acrobat in the tops of trees, using its tail to grip the branches. The kinkajou is also known as the honey bear because it often laps up the honey from bees' nests.

Kinkajou (*Potos flavus*)
Body length: up to 22 in
Tail: up to 22 in

Thick vegetation covers the highland areas on the island of Jamaica.

RESPLENDENT QUETZAL

OCELOT

KINKAJOU

GULF OF HONDURAS

RED HOWLER MONKEY

CENTRAL AMERICA

VAMPIRE BAT

Lake Managua

Lake Nicaragua

FER-DE-LANCE SNAKE

GLASS FROG

TRAP-JAW ANT

GOLDEN BEETLE

PACIFIC OCEAN

GULF OF PANAMA

CARIBBEAN SEA

CUBA

BEE HUMMINGBIRD

SOLENODON

JAMAICA

BAH

Sacred bird

The ancient peoples of Central America worshipped the brilliantly colored quetzal as the god of the air. They used the male bird's long tail feathers in their religious ceremonies. The male sheds his tail feathers after each breeding season and grows new ones the following year.

Resplendent quetzal
(*Pharomachrus mocinno*)
Body length: up to 8 in
Tail: up to 2 ft 6 in

St. Vincent parrot
(*Amazona guildingi*)
Length: 15in
Wingspan: 2 ft

Handy feet

This parrot lives only on the Caribbean island of St. Vincent. Parrots have unusual feet, with two toes pointing forward and two pointing backward. This gives them a powerful grip on branches and allows them to use their feet like hands. Each parrot is either right- or left-footed.

Scarlet ibis
(*Eudocimus ruber*)
Length: 2 ft 1 in
Wingspan: 2 ft 11 in

Curved bill

The scarlet ibis has a long, curved bill which it uses to probe in soft mud for insects, crustaceans, frogs, and fishes. Ibises feed and nest in flocks. They often nest in trees or in areas surrounded by water, where they are safer from predators. The island of Trinidad is famous for its nesting colonies.

Spotted cat

The beautiful ocelot has become very rare because its forest home is being destroyed and because it is hunted for its fur. Each cat has a different pattern of markings on its coat. The ocelot is an excellent climber and swimmer. It comes out at night to hunt for birds, snakes, and small mammals.

Rare animal

The solenodon is a rare animal that lives only in Cuba and Hispaniola. It is related to the hedgehog, and is in danger of becoming extinct because it reproduces slowly. It is also threatened by predators, such as the mongoose, which humans imported to kill snakes.

Solenodon (*Solenodon cubanus*)
Body length: up to 13 in
Tail: up to 10 in

Ocelot
(*Felis pardalis*)
Body length: up to 4 ft 3 in
Tail: up to 15 in

Loudest animal

Male red howler monkeys are the noisiest land animals in the world. Each group shouts and roars at its neighbors to keep them at a proper distance. The red howler has a large voice box, which enables it to roar so loudly that it can be heard up to 3 miles away.

Red howler monkey
(*Alouatta seniculus*)
Body length: up to 3 ft
Tail: up to 3 ft

Golden beetle
(*Plusiotis resplendens*)
Length: up to 1.5 in

Shiny wings

The metallic sheen on the wing cases of the golden beetle acts as a form of camouflage. The wing cases reflect the light and make it hard for predators to see the beetle's outline.

MARTINIQUE

BARBADOS

GUADELOUPE

ST. VINCENT PARROT

TRINIDAD

SCARLET IBIS

PUERTO RICO

HISPANIOLA

B A H A M A S

S O U T H   A M E R I C A

Many of the islands were formed by underwater volcanoes. There are still active volcanoes in the region.

Many of the Caribbean islands have sandy beaches and are popular holiday resorts.

MILES
0   100   200

The Galápagos

THE GALÁPAGOS ISLANDS lie in the Pacific Ocean, about 600 miles west of South America. They are home to a great variety of unique or unusual animals, which originally swam, flew, or drifted across to the islands from the Americas. Few mammals managed this crossing, so the islands are dominated by birds and by such reptiles as iguanas and giant tortoises. In fact the name Galápagos comes from the Spanish word for "tortoise," *galápago*.

In 1835 the British naturalist Charles Darwin visited the Galápagos. He noticed slight differences among animals of the same kind that lived on different islands. From such observations he concluded that over many generations animals change, or evolve, to take best advantage of their habitat. He developed the theory of evolution, which became a principle of modern biology.

The prickly pear is one of the few plants that can grow on the lava fields.

The Galápagos Islands were formed by underwater volcanoes and are made of volcanic lava.

The smaller Galápagos islands are largely waterless, and few plants can survive there.

FLIGHTLESS CORMORANT

FERNANDINA ISLAND
La Cumbre Volcano

LAND IGUANA

Wolf Volcano

GALÁPAGOS PENGUIN

Darwin Volcano

I S A B E L A   I S L A N D

Alcedo Volcano

Santo Tomás Volcano

MARINE IGUANA

SALLYLIGHTFOOT CRAB

PINTA ISLAND

SAN SALVADOR ISLAND

GALÁPAGOS FUR SEAL

WOODPECKER FINCH

GIANT TORTOISE

SANTA MARÍA ISLAND

SANTA CRUZ ISLAND

VERMILION FLYCATCHER

SANTA FÉ ISLAND

MARCHENA ISLAND

GENOVESA ISLAND

P A C I F I C   O C E A N

MILES
0
5
10
15

Fearless footwork
Large numbers of sallylightfoot crabs live on the rocky shores of the Galápagos. The crab has a hard shell for protection. As it grows, it sheds its shell from time to time and grows a larger one. Crabs usually run sideways to avoid tripping over their own legs. Their front legs have developed into a pair of pincers for grasping food.

Sallylightfoot crab
(*Grapsus grapsus*)
Width of shell: 4 in

Land iguana
(*Conolophus subcristatus*)
Length: over 3 ft 3 in

Fighting males
During the mating season, the male land iguana defends his territory against other males. If a rival approaches, he bobs his head in a ritual display to warn the intruder to keep away. If this does not work, a fight may break out, with the iguanas trying to bite each other with their strong teeth. They rarely fight to the death, though, and the weaker male usually retreats when he realizes he cannot win.

Useless wings
The flightless cormorant originally flew to the Galápagos. It has since lost the power of flight, probably because it had no enemies to escape from before people settled on the islands. Its wings are only one-third of the size they would have to be to support it in flight. The cormorant dives under water to catch fish. Its feathers are not waterproof, so after diving the bird has to spread its wings in the sun to dry them.

Flightless cormorant
(*Nannopterum harrisi*)
Length: 3 ft 3 in

Trusty tools

The woodpecker finch is one of the few animals that use a tool. This bird feeds on insect grubs that live under the bark or inside the trunks of trees, and it uses a twig or a cactus spine to dig them out. The woodpecker finch may even make the tool itself by breaking a twig to the right length.

Woodpecker finch
(*Camarhynchus pallidus*)
Length: 6 in

Blue-footed booby
(*Sula nebouxi*)
Length: 2 ft 10 in
Wingspan: up to
5 ft 8 in

Blue shoes

The blue-footed booby lifts its feet up and down in a comical courtship dance. The name "booby" comes from the Spanish word *bobo*, meaning "clown." The booby feeds on fish, which it catches underwater in its long, jagged bill. It often plunges into the sea from a great height to catch a fish.

Galápagos fur seal
(*Arctocephalus galapagoensis*)
Length: up to 5 ft 10 in

Fly catcher

The vermilion flycatcher often perches on the back of a giant tortoise so that it can snap up flies disturbed by the tortoise's feet. The male bird has bright red feathers, which he shows off by flying overhead in a display to attract a mate.

Vermilion flycatcher
(*Pyrocephalus rubinus*)
Length: 6 in

Fur coats

The Galápagos fur seal has a thick fur coat, which consists of an outer layer of long "guard" hairs and an inner layer of soft underfur. These seals were hunted almost to extinction so their skins could be made into fur coats for people. They are now a protected species and their numbers are beginning to increase.

Giant tortoise
(*Geochelone elephantopus*)
Shell length: 4 ft

Sea lizard

The marine iguana is the only lizard in the world that swims and feeds in the sea. It has a short snout, which enables it to gnaw seaweed off underwater rocks. Its strong claws enable it to grip the slippery rocks.

Marine iguana
(*Amblyrhynchus cristatus*)
Length: up to 4 ft

Pirate of the air

The frigate bird is named after a ship called a frigate, which was often used by pirates. When it sees another bird carrying food, the frigate bird flies after it and forces it to drop the food. Then it swoops down and grabs the stolen food in mid-air. During courtship, the male frigate bird puffs out his red throat-pouch to attract a female.

Magnificent frigate bird
(*Fregata magnificens*)
Length: 3 ft 3 in
Wingspan: up to 8 ft

Unique penguin

The Galápagos penguin is the only penguin found on the equator. Most other penguins live in Antarctica. It can survive in the Galápagos because of a water current that sweeps past the islands carrying cold water from the Antarctic.

Galápagos penguin
(*Spheniscus mendiculus*)
Height: 21 in

Super shells

The Galápagos are home to several different species of giant tortoise, which live on different islands. Each species has developed a slightly different shell shape to suit its habitat and diet. Giant tortoises have been able to survive on the islands because they can go for long periods without food or water and can move easily over rough ground. A giant tortoise may live to be over 100 years old.

MAGNIFICENT FRIGATE BIRD

SAN CRISTÓBAL ISLAND

BLUE-FOOTED BOOBY

ESPAÑOLA ISLAND

The Andes

THE ANDES are the longest chain of mountains in the world. They stretch right down the western side of South America, from the Caribbean Sea in the north to Cape Horn in the south. The Andes are among the youngest mountains on Earth. Many of the mountains in the range are volcanic, and some of them are active. Below the peaks of the Andes lie high plateaus, studded with lakes. To the east, the land slopes gently downward to the grasslands of the pampas and the rainforests of the Amazon basin.

Animals that live in these mountains have to cope with the thin air found at high altitudes. Some of them have developed extralarge hearts and lungs to help them get enough oxygen from the air. The temperature in the Andes drops to around 14°F at night, and animals such as the vicuna and alpaca have thick coats to keep them warm.

Whistling guard

Most vicunas live in a small family group that is fiercely guarded by an adult male. If the male spots any sign of danger, he whistles a loud alarm and stands guard while the females and young escape. Vicunas live high in the Andes and have thick fur coats to keep them warm.

Vicuna
(*Vicugna vicugna*)
Height at shoulder: up to 3 ft 3 in
Body length: up to 5 ft 2 in

Handy nose

The Andean tapir lives in the mountain forests. Its snout and upper lip are joined together to form a short trunk which it uses both for sniffing and for tearing leaves off branches. Tapirs are hunted by many other animals, including the jaguar, and must always be on the lookout for danger.

Andean tapir
(*Tapirus pinchaque*)
Body length: 6 ft 6 in

Digging bird

The dark-faced ground tyrant digs a long underground burrow with a nesting chamber at the end. The bird uses its beak as a pickaxe and clears away the soil with its sharp claws. The ground tyrant runs quickly along the mountain slopes on its long legs, snatching insects from the ground.

Dark-faced ground tyrant
(*Muscisaxicola macloviana*)
Length: 6 in
Wingspan: 8 in

Darwin's frog
(*Rhinoderma darwini*)
Length: up to 1 in

Frogs in the throat

The male Darwin's frog carries his tadpoles in huge pouches in his throat. This keeps them safe from predators. While the tadpoles are in his throat, the frog can make only a faint call. After about three weeks, the tadpoles change into tiny froglets and the male spits them out. The female frog plays no part in rearing the young.

Smallest deer

The pudu is the smallest deer on the American continent. It is only 15 inches high. The pudu lives in remote areas of the mountain lowlands and is very shy. This makes it hard to observe, and very little is known about its behavior. It probably lives in small groups and feeds on leaves, shoots, and fruit.

Pudu
(*Pudu mephistopheles*)
Body length: 2 ft 2 in

Wide wings

The Andean condor is one of the largest flying birds that has ever lived. It has huge wings and can soar and glide for long distances. The condor eats carrion, the flesh of dead animals. Its head and neck are bald, so it can reach into a carcass without dirtying any feathers.

Andean condor
(*Vultur gryphus*)
Wingspan: up to 10 ft

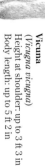

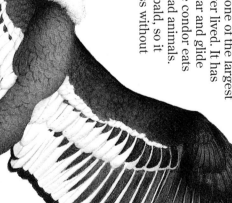

SOUTH AMERICA

Amazon

A M A Z O N   B A S I N

The Andes range contains 50 peaks that are over 19,700 feet high.

ANDEAN CONDOR

A N D E S

GROUND TYRANT

SPECTACLED BEAR

Lake Titicaca

A variety of birds and animals live in the rushes around Lake Titicaca and feed in the lake itself.

DARWIN'S FROG

TORRENT DUCK

CHINCHILLA

VICUÑA

ANDEAN TAPIR

Salado

Paraná

ALPACA

GIANT HUMMINGBIRD

A N D E S   M T S

Colorado

ANDEAN FLICKER

PUDU

P A M P A S

P A T A G O N I A

Parinacota is one of the many active volcanoes in the Andes.

A T L A N T I C   O C E A N

FALKLAND ISLANDS

TIERRA DEL FUEGO

CAPE HORN

P A C I F I C   O C E A N

MILES
0   200   400

Torrent duck
(*Merganetta armata*)
Length: 17 in

Biggest hummingbird

The Andean giant hummingbird is the largest hummingbird in the world. During the cold mountain nights, its body temperature falls to just above that of the air. This helps the bird to save energy, which it would otherwise use up trying to keep warm.

Giant hummingbird
(*Patagona gigas*)
Length: 8.5 in

Chiseling beak

The Andean flicker is a type of woodpecker. It uses its strong beak to chisel out a nesting hole in the spiny leaves of a puya plant. The flicker's feet are specially adapted for climbing, with two toes pointing forward and two backward. Its curved claws give it an extra grip.

Andean flicker
(*Colaptes rupicola*)
Length: 12 in

Furry coat

Chinchillas live high up in the Andes and have soft, thick fur coats that keep out the cold. Many of them have been killed for their fur, which is used to make coats and jackets, and they are now rare animals. Chinchillas make their homes in holes and cracks among the rocks.

Chinchilla (*Chinchilla laniger*)
Body length: up to 15 in
Tail: up to 6 in

Changing spectacles

The white markings around the eyes of the spectacled bear make it look as if it is wearing spectacles. These markings vary a lot, and each animal has different-shaped spectacles. The bear is a good climber. At night it sleeps in a tree, where it builds a rough nest of sticks.

Spectacled bear
(*Tremarctos ornatus*)
Height at shoulder: 2 ft 6 in
Body length: up to 5 ft 10 in

Waterfall duck

The torrent duck feeds in the fast-flowing streams of the Andes, where there are many waterfalls and rapids. It uses its sharp claws to grip slippery boulders and steers its way through the rushing waters, using its stiff tail as a rudder. Its streamlined body shape helps it to swim underwater when it dives to look for food.

Shaggy camel

The alpaca is a relative of the camel. It has a shaggy coat of fine, soft hair that reaches almost to the ground. People farm alpacas like sheep, cutting off their woolly coats to make clothes. An alpaca's fleece weighs about 6.5 pounds.

Alpaca (*Lama pacos*)
Height at shoulder: 4 ft
Body length: 4 ft

Amazon Rainforest

THE VAST AMAZON JUNGLE is the largest area of tropical rainforest in the world. It covers about 2,700,000 square miles – an area 12 times the size of France. The rainforest is situated in the huge basin of the Amazon River, which flows 4,000 miles across South America. The weather in the Amazon basin is hot and humid all year round.

The Amazon rainforest is home to a greater variety of wildlife than anywhere else on Earth. Many animals live in the treetops, where there are plenty of leaves, flowers, and fruit to feed on. Some animals have grasping tails and long claws to help them swing through the branches; others have membranes of skin that unfold as they glide from branch to branch. Rainforest birds often have short wings that allow them to fly through the trees. On the forest floor, many animals find food with their long noses and sharp digging claws. Today large areas of the rainforest are being cleared for farming and mining, and many of the animals and plants are threatened.

Reflecting wings

Because of the way the tiny scales on its wings reflect the light. As the butterfly moves its wings, the colors change. Many morphos have been collected for jewelry or decoration, and they are in danger of becoming extinct.

The male morpho butterfly is brilliantly colored

Blue morpho butterfly
(*Morpho rhetenor*)
Wingspan: up to 7 in

Toco toucan
(*Ramphastos toco*)
Length: 2 ft
Bill: 10 in

Biggest bill

The toco toucan has the biggest bill of any bird. But its bill is lighter than it looks. Both parts are hollow, with thin rods of bone inside for support. With its long bill, the toucan can reach fruit on twigs too thin to bear its weight.

(*Opisthocomus hoatzin*)
Length: up to 2 ft 2 in
Hoatzin

Weak wings

The hoatzin has such weak flight muscles that it cannot fly more than 330 feet or so before it has to crash-land for a rest. It uses its wings and tail for extra support as it climbs through the trees. The hoatzin feeds on tough mangrove and arum leaves.

Underwater danger

The caiman is a type of crocodile. It lurks underwater with just its nose and eyes showing. When a thirsty animal comes for a drink, the caiman snaps it up with its sharp teeth and holds it underwater until it drowns.

Spectacled caiman
(*Caiman crocodylus*)
Length including tail:
up to 15 ft

Acrobatic leaps

The spider monkey is an amazing acrobat. It makes leaps of 30 feet or more through the trees. Its tail grasps and coils around the branches like an extra hand or arm. Such a tail is called a prehensile tail. A patch of skin on the underside of the tail secures a firm grip.

Spider monkey
(*Ateles geoffroyi*)
Body length:
up to 2 ft
Tail: up to 3 ft

Spotted cat

The jaguar is the largest cat in South America. Unlike the leopard, it has black marks inside each ring of spots. Its coat acts as camouflage in the forest, and it can creep up on the animals it hunts without being seen.

Jaguar (*Panthera onca*)
Height at shoulder: 2 ft 4 in
Body length: up to 5 ft 9 in

The highest parts of the rainforest receive up to 120 inches of rain each year.

PACIFIC OCEAN

ANDES MTS

GULF OF PANAMA

CARIBBEAN

Lake Maracaibo

S

A

M

Amazon

HARPY EAGLE

SLOTH

SCARLET MACAW

Nutcracker beak

The scarlet macaw is the largest of the South American parrots and has the longest tail. Its strong, hooked beak has scissorlike cutting edges which work like massive nutcrackers. Its beak is so strong that it can split open the tough shells of Brazil nuts. The macaw often uses one of its feet as a "hand" to hold food up to its mouth.

Scarlet macaw
(*Ara macao*)
Body length: 12 in
Tail feathers: 2 ft

Red piranha
(*Serrasalmus nattereri*)
Length: up to 2 ft

Razor teeth

Piranhas have powerful jaws with razor-sharp teeth. When hundreds of them attack together, they can kill and strip a large animal in minutes.

Emerald tree boa
(*Corallus caninus*)
Length: up to 6 ft

Deadly embrace

The emerald tree boa is not poisonous; it uses its powerful muscles to squeeze its prey to death. The tree boa is well camouflaged among the leaves. Its bright green skin helps it to hide from predators, such as the harpy eagle, and allows it to move close to its prey before it strikes.

Harpy eagle
(*Harpia harpyja*)
Length: 3 ft 3 in

Biggest eagle

The harpy eagle is the largest and most powerful eagle in the world. It flies at speeds of up to 50 mph as it chases monkeys and other animals through the treetops. Its feet are about the size of a human hand and are tipped with sharp, curved talons. Once these claws grip an animal, it has little chance of escape.

Hummingbird
(*Chrysolampis mosquitus*)
Length: up to 3 in

Hovering jewels

The ruby-topaz hummingbird hovers in front of the forest flowers for nectar as it probes with its long bill. Its wings beat as fast as 80 times per second. It can hover in one place and even fly backward. It does not need to be camouflaged, as it can fly off at speeds of up to 40 mph.

Giant armadillo
(*Priodontes giganteus*)
Body length: 3 ft 3 in

Largest claws

The giant armadillo is about the size of a sheep. At night, it uses its huge, curved claws to dig for worms, ants, termites, and snakes on the forest floor. The claws on its front feet are the largest of any living animal.

Sloth
(*Bradypus tridactylus*)
Length: up to 2 ft

Upside-down life

The sloth uses its long, hooklike claws to hang upside down from branches. It may stay in the same tree for years. Its fur grows down from its stomach to its back so that rain runs off more easily. In the rainy season, the sloth turns green because of the microscopic green algae that live in its fur.

ATLANTIC OCEAN

BRAZILIAN HIGHLANDS

The Amazon River is fed by over 1,000 tributaries.

MOUTHS OF THE AMAZON

MILES
0   200   400

S O U T H   A M E R I C A

ORINOCO

HOATZIN

BLUE MORPHO BUTTERFLY

JAGUAR

CAIMAN

HUMMINGBIRD

SPIDER MONKEY

Rio Negro

Amazon

Jurua

RED PIRANHA

EMERALD TREE BOA

GIANT ARMADILLO

TOCO TOUCAN

The Amazon Basin is home to over 100,000 species of plants.

Lake Titicaca

SEA

The Pampas

THE PAMPAS IS A VAST GRASSY plain that covers an area of almost 300,000 square miles in South America. The climate in the pampas is generally dry. Although grasses flourish in these conditions, trees and larger plants can survive only along river banks. Termite mounds, which can be more than 6 feet high, dot the pampas landscape.

Many pampas animals, such as the armadillo, live in underground burrows. This protects them from the fires that are common on the dry grassland. Much of the pampas is now used by farmers for grazing cattle. Many of the wild animals therefore face extra competition for food, and some species are declining as a result.

Ovenbird
(*Furnarius rufus*)
Length: up to 8 in

Baker bird
The ovenbird is named after its nest, which looks like a round earthenware oven. There are few trees on the pampas, so the nest is often situated on a post instead. The female bird builds the nest from up to 2,500 lumps of mud.

Gray rhea
(*Rhea americana*)
Height: up to 5 ft

Speedy sprinter
The rhea is a flightless bird. It can run at speeds of more than 30 mph. The male rhea rears the chicks and defends the nest. He will attack anything that comes too close, even people and small airplanes.

Pampas deer
(*Odocoileus bezoarticus*)
Height at shoulder: 2 ft 3 in
Body length: 4 ft

Rare deer
The pampas deer is one of the few large plant-eating animals left on the grasslands. It is now rare, due to hunting and competition from grazing cattle. Glands on the back hooves of the male give off an odor that can be detected more than a mile away.

Pink fairy armadillo
(*Chlamyphorus truncatus*)
Body length: up to 6 in

Chain mail
The pink fairy armadillo has protective armor on its back, made of plates of bone covered with horny scales. It uses the huge claws on its front feet for digging. Because it spends a lot of time underground, the armadillo's eyes are tiny and its sight is poor.

Viscacha
(*Lagostomus maximus*)
Body length: up to 2 ft 2 in
Tail: up to 8 in

Underground city
Viscachas are rodents that dig huge networks of tunnels under the pampas. Many generations of viscachas may live in the same burrow. Other animals, such as maras and burrowing owls, often live in viscacha burrows. The viscacha digs mainly with its front feet, pushing the soil out of the way with its nose. It can close its nostrils to stop soil from getting in.

Crested caracara
(*Polyborus plancus*)
Length: up to 2 ft

Bullying bird
The crested caracara is a bird of prey. It eats insects and other small animals, but it also likes carrion, the flesh of dead animals. The caracara sometimes pecks and bullies a vulture until it forces it to cough up some of the carrion it has just eaten.

Mara (*Dolichotis patagona*)
Body length: up to 2 ft 6 in

Long jump
The mara, or Patagonian hare, has long back legs which it uses to bound away from danger. It can cover nearly 7 feet in one leap. Although the mara looks like a hare, it is related to the guinea pig. Mara young are raised in burrows, in groups of up to 40.

MILES

0   150   300

Camouflage colors

The mottled patterns on the crested tinamou's feathers serve to camouflage it on the open grasslands. The tinamou has powerful legs and can run fast for short distances, but it soon becomes tired. It is not good at flying and often collides with obstacles. The bird lays brightly colored eggs in a hollow on the ground.

Crested tinamou
(*Eudromia elegans*)
Length: up to 21 in

Long-legged wolf

The maned wolf has long legs which enable it to move easily through the long grass of the pampas. If a maned wolf is threatened by an enemy, the mane of hair on its neck and shoulders stands up to make it look bigger and more frightening. It hunts at night for small mammals, birds, reptiles, and insects.

Maned wolf
(*Chrysocyon brachyurus*)
Body length: 4 ft
Tail: 12 in

Terrific tongue

The giant anteater feeds on ants and termites, which it licks up with its long, sticky tongue. A giant anteater may have to visit 40 termite mounds in one hour to find enough food to eat. It rips open the mounds with its huge claws. The anteater sleeps in the open and wraps its hairy tail over its body like a blanket.

Cavy (*Cavia aperea*)
Body length: up to 16 in

Sharp claws

The cavy is the wild ancestor of the guinea pig that some people keep as a pet. The cavy has sharp claws and is a good digger, but it often prefers to use burrows made by other animals or to shelter under rocks. Cavies usually live in small groups but sometimes hundreds of them live together in a suitable area.

Giant anteater
(*Myrmecophaga tridactyla*)
Body length: up to 4 ft
Tail: up to 3 ft

Burrowing owl
(*Speotyto cunicularia*)
Length: 18 in

Daytime owl

Unlike most other owls, the burrowing owl hunts during the day. It perches on the mounds of soil dug out by viscachas, watching for insects or other small animals to stir in the grass. Its long legs help it to run fast over the ground and catch its food. This owl nests in an underground burrow.

SOUTH AMERICA

Uruguay

Paraná

Rio de la Plata

OVENBIRD

VISCACHA

CRESTED TINAMOU

MANED WOLF

GIANT ANTEATER

PAMPAS DEER

P A M P A S

PINK FAIRY ARMADILLO

GRAY RHEA

CAVY

MARA

BURROWING OWL

CRESTED CARACARA

Negro

Salado

A N D E S   M T S

P A M P A S

P A C I F I C   O C E A N

A T L A N T I C   O C E A N

Some pampas grasses can grow to a height of 8 feet.

Today large areas of the pampas are used by farmers for raising beef cattle.

The lack of trees and bushes on the pampas means that many animals and birds have to take cover in underground burrows.

Conifer Forests

A THICK BAND OF DENSE EVERGREEN FOREST stretches across the northern parts of Europe, covering large areas of the northern British Isles and Scandinavia. There are smaller evergreen forests farther south, such as the Black Forest in Germany and the Ardennes in Belgium. The most common trees in all these forests are conifers – trees that have cones – such as pine, spruce, and fir. A thick layer of their needles covers the ground. In recent years acid rain, which is especially harmful to evergreen trees, has damaged many European forests.

Animals that live in these forests have to survive in a severe climate. The winters are bitterly cold, but conifer trees keep their leaves all year round and provide some shelter from the worst of the weather. Some forest animals grow white coats in the winter so that they are camouflaged against the snow. Other animals, such as the long-eared bat and the wood ant, hibernate during the winter months and avoid the worst of the weather. Many birds, such as the osprey, migrate south to warmer countries.

Long ears
The long-eared bat's huge ears are three-quarters the length of its body. They are so big that a young bat cannot hold its ears up straight until it is old enough to fly. The bat feeds on moths, midges, and flies, often swooping down to pick them off plants. During the cold winter months, the long-eared bat usually hibernates in a cave.

Long-eared bat
(*Plecotus auritus*)
Body length: up to 2 in
Wingspan: up to 11 in

Under a blanket
Wood ants build huge mounds on the forest floor from pine needles and other plant material. The mounds keep the ground warm in winter, while the ants hibernate in the soil below. If it is threatened, a wood ant sprays its enemy with a stinging liquid called formic acid from glands on its abdomen. People can see and smell this chemical. The wood ant eats all kinds of other insects and may catch some of them high up in the trees.

Wood ant (*Formica rufa*)
Length: 0.5 in

Ringed tail
The wild cat is closely related to the domestic cat but it is slightly bigger and has a thicker tail with black rings on it. The wild cat hunts at night for small mammals, birds, and insects. The forests provide it with cover for hunting.

Wild cat (*Felis sylvestris*)
Body length: up to 2 ft 6 in
Tail: up to 15 in

Crossed beak
The crossbill uses its chunky, crossed beak to tear open pine cones. Then it licks out the seeds with its horny tongue. Adult crossbills regurgitate (spit up) partly digested seeds to feed their young. Every few years, crossbills move out of their usual breeding areas and invade other parts of Europe in enormous numbers. If conditions are favorable, they settle in the new area for one or more seasons.

Common crossbill
(*Loxia curvirostra*)
Length: 6.5 in

False ears
The "ears" of the long-eared owl are only tufts of feathers. Its real ear openings are on the sides of its head. The owl hunts at night, using its sharp eyesight and good hearing to find small mammals on the woodland floor.

Long-eared owl
(*Asio otus*)
Length: 13 in
Wingspan: 3 ft

Fish snatcher
The osprey feeds on fish which it snatches from lakes. Its long, sharp claws and the horny spines under its toes enable it to grip a slippery fish. An adult osprey can carry a fish of 4 pounds or more, heavier than itself. In autumn, the European osprey migrates to Africa, where it is warmer and there are plenty of fish.

Osprey (*Pandion haliaetus*)
Length: up to 2 ft
Wingspan: up to 5 ft 4 in

Ichneumon fly
(*Rhyssa persuasoria*)
Length: 2 in

Capercaillie
(*Tetrao urogallus*)
Length: up to
2 ft 10 in

Dancing display

In spring, the male capercaillie puts on a strange display to attract females. He fans out his tail, points his neck upward, and makes gurgling sounds. He may even jump into the air and clap his wings. Displaying capercaillies are very aggressive and may threaten deer, sheep, or even humans who disturb them.

Eaten alive

The female ichneumon lays her eggs inside the larvae of wood wasps. When the young grubs hatch, they feed on the wood wasp larvae. Because the wasp larvae tunnel deep inside tree trunks, the ichneumon drills through the wood with its egg-laying tube, which is almost as long as its body.

Flying acrobat

The pine marten is an acrobatic and swift nighttime hunter. It hunts on the ground and in the trees and often "flies" from tree to tree as it chases its prey. Its powerful legs, broad pads, and long claws make it a good climber, and its bushy tail enables it to balance. The pine marten has a varied diet and eats anything from small birds and their eggs to rats, beetles, and wild fruits.

Pine marten (*Martes martes*)
Body length: up to 20 in

Antler fights

In the autumn breeding season, called the rut, the males of the red deer fight with their antlers. Those with large antlers win females for mating. Each male sheds his antlers in the next breeding season. During the rut, the male spends his time roaring, fighting rivals, and rounding up females.

Red deer
(*Cervus elaphus*)
Height at shoulder:
up to 5 ft 7 in
Length: up to 8 ft 2 in

Smelly protection

If it is threatened, the polecat produces a foul-smelling liquid from glands under its tail. The polecat also uses this special odor to mark its territory. The scent marks tell other polecats to stay away. Polecats do not hibernate. They hunt for small mammals all year round.

European polecat
(*Mustela putorius*)
Body length:
up to 18 in

Winters in the forests are bitterly cold, with snow covering the ground for up to half the year.

Many European conifer forests have been planted and are harvested for their timber.

The many lakes in the northern European forests provide animals with places to drink.

Lake Onega

Lake Ladoga

PINE MARTEN

COMMON CROSSBILL

OSPREY

LONG-EARED BAT

LONG-EARED OWL

S C A N D I N A V I A

N O R T H E R N

BALTIC SEA

Wisla

Oder

E U R O P E

N O R T H SEA

ICHNEUMON FLY

ARDENNES FOREST

BLACK FOREST

Danube

RED DEER

ENGLISH CHANNEL

WILD CAT

CAPERCAILLIE

WOOD ANT

B R I T I S H I S L E S

EUROPEAN POLECAT

MILES
0   100   200

Woodlands

THE WOODLANDS of Europe provide food and shelter for a rich and varied community of wildlife. Every tree supports its own web of life. Insects feed on the leaves, birds and mammals nest in the trunk and branches, and creatures such as woodlice and beetles live in the leaf litter on the woodland floor.

The weather changes with the seasons, and this affects the behavior and lifestyle of the animals. In the warm spring days insects emerge, birds begin to nest, and the young of mammals are born. In the hot summer months there is plenty of food, and the young animals grow quickly. In the fall most of the trees lose their leaves, and the animals feast on fruits and berries or store food for the winter. The long, cold nights and short days make winter a difficult time for the animals. Many grow thick coats and spend more time in their burrows or tree holes. Some birds fly away to spend the winter months in warmer climates.

Strong digger

Badgers have strong front legs and long, sharp claws which they use to dig out extensive burrows, called sets. The tunnels of European badgers can be up to 65 feet long. Generations of badgers may live in the same set for hundreds of years. When digging, badgers can close their ears and nostrils to keep out dirt.

European badger
(*Meles meles*)
Body length: 2 ft 6 in
Tail: 6 in

Summer spots

Fallow deer have white spots in summer; in the winter their coats turn darker and the spots are hard to see. The young have striped coats which make them hard to see and protect them from predators.

Fallow deer (*Dama dama*)
Height at shoulder: 4 ft 5 in
Body length: 5 ft 2 in

Super snout

The wild boar is the ancestor of the domestic pig. It uses its long, sensitive nose to search along the woodland floor for roots, bulbs, nuts, mushrooms, and small creatures.

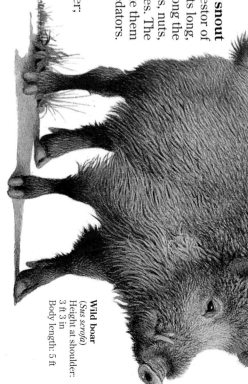

Wild boar (*Sus scrofa*)
Height at shoulder: 3 ft 3 in
Body length: 5 ft

Antler jaws

Male stag beetles have jaws that look like stags' antlers. They use these jaws to fight rivals. Females lay their eggs in rotting wood, which the larvae feed on until they grow into adults.

Stag beetle
Length including antlers: up to 3 in

Nutcracker beak

The nuthatch can wedge a nut in the bark of a tree and hammer it open with its sharp beak. It is the only bird that can climb head first down trees. As it moves up and down the trunk, it searches for insects under the bark.

Nuthatch (*Sitta europaea*)
Length: 6 in

Caterpillar diet

In spring and summer, blue tits feed their young mainly on caterpillars. While the young are in the nest, their parents may bring them more than 10,000 items of food. In winter blue tits feed in mixed flocks with treecreepers, great tits, and other small birds.

Blue tit (*Parus caeruleus*)
Length: 5 in

ATLANTIC OCEAN

BRITISH ISLES

IRISH SEA

BLUE TIT

BADGER

NUTHATCH

WEASEL

STAG BEETLE

GREAT SPOTTED WOODPECKER

ENGLISH CHANNEL

Loire

PYRENEES

Rhône

WILD BOAR

NORTH SEA

E

Northern Europe has a mild climate and plentiful supplies of water.

Tree acrobat

The red squirrel's long, bushy tail helps it to balance as it leaps from tree to tree. The squirrel may also use its tail to signal to other squirrels, flicking it to warn them of danger. The squirrel has long, strong back legs and hooked claws, which help it to grip tree bark. Red squirrels usually climb down a tree head first.

Red squirrel (*Sciurus vulgaris*)
Body length: 10 in
Tail: 8 in

Prickly armor

A hedgehog has up to 5,000 spines on its back. Spines are really modified hairs. Although they are hollow, they are very strong and have sharp points. If a hedgehog is alarmed, it rolls into a ball to protect its underparts with its spines. Baby hedgehogs have soft spines so they do not scratch their mothers while suckling.

European hedgehog
(*Erinaceus europaeus*)
Length: 9 in

Clinging claws

The great spotted woodpecker has sharp, curved claws that help it cling tightly to tree bark. Its stiff tail feathers help to support its weight against the trunk. With its powerful, straight beak the woodpecker chisels insects out from under the bark. It uses its long, sticky tongue to reach into cracks and crevices and lick up insects.

Great spotted woodpecker
(*Dendrocopos major*)
Length: 9 in

Tawny owl (*Strix aluco*)
Length: 1 ft 3 in
Wingspan: 3 ft 3 in

Silent wings

The tawny owl hunts at night. It has soft, fringed wing feathers which are specially suited for silent flying. It can see well in the dark and has very good hearing. Its prey are small creatures, such as mice and voles, which it seizes with its curved talons.

Common dormouse
(*Muscardinus avellanarius*)
Body length: 3 in
Tail: 2.5 in

Night hunter

Red foxes hunt mainly at night. They eat almost anything, from rabbits and earthworms to fish and apples. In towns they even search in people's garbage cans for food. To catch a mouse, a fox will often leap straight up and then pin the mouse to the ground with its front paws.

Red fox (*Vulpes vulpes*)
Height to shoulder: 14 in
Body length: 2 ft 5 in

Winter sleeper

Dormice hibernate (sleep) through the cold winter months in a warm nest of leaves and grass. The nest may be under leaf litter or in a hollow tree stump. Dormice eat as much as possible in the fall and may nearly double in weight. This helps them to survive during hibernation.

Weasel (*Mustela nivalis*)
Body length: 8 in
Tail: 2 in

Slim hunter

Weasels have long, thin bodies which enable them to squeeze into the burrows of mice and voles and prevent them from escaping. Weasels are strong for their size and can kill much larger animals.

There are many gaps in the trees that let light down to the woodland floor.

Rotting leaves litter the woodland floor and provide a rich source of food for plants and insects.

MILES
0   100   200

TAWNY OWL

HEDGEHOG

FALLOW DEER

RED SQUIRREL

RED FOX

DORMOUSE

E U R O P E

Elbe

Rhine

Danube

A L P S

Southern Europe

THE COUNTRIES OF SOUTHERN EUROPE lie around the northern coast of the Mediterranean Sea. They have a climate of long, hot, dry summers with cooler, wetter winters. The typical landscape of this region is dry scrubland.

Large numbers of people live in southern Europe or visit the area on vacation. People have polluted the sea and destroyed most of the forests that once covered the region. But there are still some refuges for wildlife, such as the Alps and Pyrenees mountains and the marshlands of the Coto Doñana in Spain and the Camargue in France. Some rare animals, such as the chamois and the Spanish lynx, live in these protected areas. Southern Europe is also famous for its bird life. Huge numbers of storks, buzzards, eagles, and songbirds travel across the region on their regular migration routes between Europe and Africa.

Brown bear (*Ursus arctos*)
Height at shoulder: up to 3 ft
Head and body: up to 6 ft 6 in

Chamois (*Rupicapra rupicapra*)
Height at shoulder: up to 2 ft 8 in
Length: 4 ft

Short-sighted bear
The brown bear of southern Europe lives in the mountains. Bears are short-sighted, so they rely on their keen sense of smell to find food. The brown bear is mostly vegetarian and uses its long claws to dig up roots, shoots, and bulbs. In the fall, the bear fattens up on fruits and berries to last it through the winter, when it hibernates.

Green toad (*Bufo viridis*)
Length: 4 in

Insect gobbler
The green toad comes out in the cool, moist night air to hunt for insects. It sometimes enters villages to hunt around street lamps and other sources of light, which attract insects. Toads have no teeth and swallow their food whole.

Hoopoe (*Upupa epops*)
Length: 11 in

Name call
The hoopoe is named after its call, which sounds like "hoo-poo-poo." Young hoopoes drive intruders away from their nest by hissing loudly, producing a strong odor, and poking their bills upward.

Olm (*Proteus anguinus*)
Length: up to 12 in

Clinging feet
The nimble, sure-footed chamois leaps about the rocky crags in mountainous areas of southern Europe. It has strong legs, and the spongy pads under its hooves can grip the steep or slippery surfaces. The chamois has an incredible sense of balance. Its leaps can be over 19 feet long and 13 feet high.

Blind cave-dweller
The olm, or cave salamander, lives in underground pools and streams. It has no eyes. It lives in pitch darkness and does not need to see. The olm breathes partly through the red gills on the sides of its head.

Lammergeier (*Gypaetus barbatus*)
Length: up to 3 ft 10 in
Wingspan: up to 9 ft

Bone breaker
The lammergeier, or bearded vulture, feeds on bones that it scavenges from dead animals. It waits until other kinds of vultures have pecked all the meat off the bones, and then it feeds. The lammergeier sometimes drops bones from a great height so they crack open. It can then get at the marrow inside.

ATLANTIC OCEAN

SPANISH LYNX

SMALL-SPOTTED GENET

ROCK OF GIBRALTAR

BARBARY APE

Douro

CHAMOIS

BROWN BEAR

BALEARIC ISLANDS

LAMMERGEIER

Garonne

GOLDEN ORIOLE

Dordogne

GREATER FLAMINGO

HOOPOE

CORSICA

SARDINIA

MEDITERRANEAN MONK SEAL

BAY OF BISCAY

SOUTHERN

ALPS

MEDI

The typical Mediterranean habitat consists of dry scrubland covered with thorny shrubs and small trees.

Spotted stalker
The small-spotted genet sleeps during the day and comes out at night to stalk small mammals, nesting birds, reptiles, and insects. Its keen eyesight, smell, and hearing make it an efficient hunter. The genet is a good climber. It uses its sharp claws to cling to tree trunks and branches.

Filter beak
The greater flamingo wades through shallow water using its webbed feet to stir up shrimps and other small shellfish from the muddy bottom. Special fringes inside the flamingo's beak filter these creatures out of the water and mud so that the bird can swallow them.

Greater flamingo
(*Phoenicopterus ruber*)
Height: 4 ft
Wingspan: 4 ft 8 in

Thread lacewing
(*Nemoptera sinuata*)
Wingspan: 2 in

Streamer wings
The male thread lacewing has long, thin back wings which trail behind him like streamers. Large groups of males dance up and down displaying their wings. This probably attracts females.

Golden oriole
(*Oriolus oriolus*)
Length: 24 cm (9.5 in)

Golden bird
The male golden oriole has bright yellow and black feathers, which help him to attract a female. The female is a drab green. This provides camouflage when she sits on the nest. In winter, golden orioles migrate to Africa.

Seal survivor
The Mediterranean monk seal is one of the rarest seals in the world. It once lived all around this sea, but the beaches where it used to rest and breed have been taken over by vacationers. There are probably only a few hundred monk seals left, and the species faces extinction.

Mediterranean monk seal
(*Monachus monachus*)
Length: up to 8 ft 10 in

Spanish lynx (*Felis lynx*)
Body length: 4 ft 3 in
Tail: 3 in

Rare cat
The Spanish lynx was once widespread but its numbers have been drastically reduced because of hunting and the destruction of its forest habitat. Today it is found only in remote mountainous areas and in the Coto Doñana reserve. The lynx lives alone and hunts for small mammals and birds at night.

Barbary ape
(*Macaca sylvanus*)
Length: up to 2 ft 6 in

Gibraltar monkey
Barbary apes live on the Rock of Gibraltar, but no one is sure how they got there. Many centuries ago the Romans may have taken them there from North Africa. Although these creatures are called apes, they are in fact a kind of monkey.

Small-spotted genet
(*Genetta genetta*)
Body length: up to 2 ft
Tail: up to 18 in

MILES
0   150   300

The Mediterranean coastline is dotted with beaches where turtles and seals come ashore to breed.

The Camargue is a marshly area in southern France, famous for its wild horses, bulls, and flamingos.

CRETE

GREEN TOAD

OLM

THREAD LACEWING

EUROPE

SICILY

M E D I T E R R A N E A N   S E A

A F R I C A

The Sahara

THE SHIFTING SANDS of the Sahara Desert stretch across 3,500,000 square miles of northern Africa, an area almost as big as the United States. The Sahara is the largest desert in the world – and it is still growing. In the baking heat of the day, the temperature soars to over 122° F in the shade. But at night it is bitterly cold. Hardly any rain falls. In some areas there may be no rain at all for several years.

The animals that live in the Sahara have adapted to this harsh environment in a variety of ways. Many small animals hide in burrows during the day and only come out at dawn and dusk, when it is cooler. Most desert animals can go for long periods without water. Some never drink – they get all the moisture they need from the plants and insects they eat.

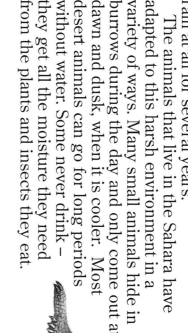

Desert hedgehog
(*Hemiechinus auritus*)
Length: 6 in

Big ears
The fennec fox has huge ears that can be up to 6 inches long. The large, thin surface of the ears allows heat to escape from the fox's body, like a radiator giving off heat. When the fox hunts, it can hear small animals moving around.

Fennec fox (*Vulpes zerda*)
Body length: up to 16 in
Tail: up to 8 in

Desert scorpion
(*Androctonus australis*)
Length: 3 in

Super sting
The desert scorpion defends itself with the sting at the end of its tail. The sting is as poisonous as the bite of a cobra and can kill a much larger animal, such as a dog, in only seven minutes.

Prickly hunter
The desert hedgehog spends the day in a burrow and hunts at night. Its long legs lift its body above the hot sand. One of the hedgehog's favorite meals is a scorpion, which it eats after first biting off the sting in its tail.

Champion jumper
The jerboa is like a tiny kangaroo. It can jump up to 8 feet in a single bound. This helps it to escape from predators. Its strong back legs are four times as long as the front legs. The long tail helps the jerboa to balance when it jumps and supports its body when it is standing still.

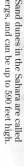
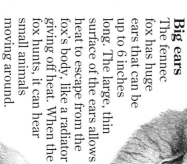

Jerboa
(*Jaculus jaculus*)
Body length:
up to 6 in
Tail: 10 in

Colorful reptile
The chameleon is a reptile and can survive in higher temperatures than birds or mammals. It can change color rapidly. The insects it catches with its long tongue provide water as well as food.

Chameleon
(*Chamaeleo chamaeleon*)
Length including tail: 9 in

Furry feet
The sand cat has thick fur under its feet. The fur helps to keep it from sinking into the soft sand and protects it from the heat of the sand. When it hunts, its large ears enable it to hear and locate animals from a long way off.

Sand cat (*Felis margarita*)
Height at shoulder: up to 9 in
Body length: up to 22 in

In the Sahara there are several hot, dry, mountainous regions where few plants and animals can survive.

Sand dunes in the Sahara are called ergs, and can be up to 590 feet high.

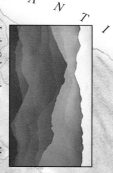

A T L A N T I C   O C E A N

A T L A S   M T S

AHAGGAR MTS

S A H A R A

A F R I C A

M E D I T

BARBARY SHEEP

SOOTY FALCON

DROMEDARY CAMEL

FENNEC FOX

DESERT HEDGEHOG

SPINY-TAILED AGAMA

Fatty hump

The dromedary or Arabian camel can go without water for a few weeks. Its hump is made up mostly of fat, which provides energy when food and water are scarce. The camel has long, thick eyelashes which protect its eyes, and can close its nostrils to keep out sand.

Addax
(*Addax nasomaculatus*)
Height at shoulder: 4 ft
Horns: up to 3 ft 6 in

Spiny-tailed agama (*Uromastix acanthinurus*)
Length including tail: 10 in

Rare addax

Many addax have been killed for their skin, so they are now quite rare. The addax never drinks. It gets all the moisture it needs from the plants it eats. Its wide hooves allow it to travel quickly and easily over soft sand.

Fat tail

The spiny-tailed agama is a type of lizard. If food is scarce, it can survive for up to a month on the fat store in its tail. The tail is ringed with sharp scales. If attacked, the agama dives into its burrow but leaves its tail sticking up at the entrance.

Fierce falcon

Sooty falcon chicks hatch in late summer. At this time of year many small birds migrate across the Sahara. The parent falcons catch birds that stop to rest and bring them to their chicks.

Dromedary camel
(*Camelus dromedarius*)
Height at shoulder: 6 ft
Body length: up to 11 ft

Sooty falcon
(*Falco araea*)
Length: 13 in

Flying water carrier

Sandgrouse need to drink water every day. The chicks cannot fly off to find water, but their father carries it to them. He flies to a waterhole and sits in the water until his belly feathers are soaked to the skin. When he returns, he stands while the chicks drink from his feathers.

Sandgrouse
(*Pterocles alchata*)
Length: 13 in

Dung roller

The scarab beetle has a thick, shiny skin which reflects the sun's rays and keeps it cool. The ancient Egyptians believed that these beetles were sacred. One common scarab eats the dung of other desert animals. It rolls the dung into balls and buries it in holes as food for its young.

Scarab beetle
(*Scarabaeus sacer*)
Length: up to 2 in

Barbary sheep (*Ammotragus lervia*)
Height at shoulder: up to 3 ft 3 in
Horns: up to 2 ft 6 in

Rock climber

Barbary sheep live in the mountains of the Sahara. They are good at climbing on the rocky crags and look more like goats than sheep. They get most of the water they need from the mountain plants they eat, so they rarely need to drink.

ARABIAN PENINSULA

RED SEA

MEDITERRANEAN SEA

Nile

Lake Nasser

TIBESTI MTS

SAHARA DESERT

CHAMELEON

SAND CAT

JERBOA

SCORPION

SCARAB BEETLE

SANDGROUSE

ADDAX

The Sahara has many rocky plateaus, called hammadas.

MILES
0   200   400   600

Rainforests and Lakes

THE TROPICAL RAINFORESTS of Africa stretch in a broad band from West Africa to the edge of the Great Rift Valley. This valley is a huge system of troughs more than 4,000 miles long that was created by movements of the Earth's crust. The floor of the Rift Valley is studded with a series of spectacular lakes which provide a rich habitat for wildlife.

The warm, humid environment of the rainforest is home to many animals, from okapis and forest birds to frogs, snakes, and insects. Many of the plant-eating animals feed on the shrubs that form a tangled mass beneath the giant forest trees. Leaves and fruits that fall to the forest floor decay rapidly, providing food for pigs, porcupines, and termites. Some forest animals are good at climbing and can reach food high in the trees. Camouflage helps many forest animals to hide from predators or to creep up on their prey without being seen. Unfortunately, large areas of rainforest have been destroyed for timber or cleared for farms and villages, and many of the animals, such as the gorilla, face possible extinction.

Royal antelope (*Neotragus pygmaeus*)
Body length: up to 2 ft 1 in
Height at shoulder: up to 12 in

Gentle giant
Gorillas are gentle vegetarians that feed on leaves, stalks, bark, and fruits. They live in close-knit groups of up to 30 members, each led by an adult male. Gorillas use a wide range of sounds and gestures to communicate with one another. For example, a male threatens his rivals by standing up and beating his chest. Male gorillas over ten years old have silvery-gray hair on their backs and are nicknamed silverbacks.

Armor plating
The tree pangolin is covered in horny scales that act as a suit of armor to protect it from predators. The pangolin uses its long tail as an extra hand to grasp the branches. Its grip is so strong that it can hang from branches by the tip of its tail alone. The pangolin feeds on ants and termites. It tears open their nests with its strong front legs and licks up the insects with its long tongue.

Tree pangolin
(*Manis tricuspis*)
Body length: up to 18 in
Tail: up to 2 ft

Gorilla
(*Gorilla gorilla*)
Height: up to 6 ft

Pencil legs
The tiny royal antelope is the size of a rabbit and its legs are as thin as pencils. It is the smallest antelope in the world. When escaping from enemies, such as larger mammals, birds, and snakes, the royal antelope can leap as far as 9 feet in one bound. The royal antelope is a shy, timid animal. It hides during the day and comes out to feed on leaves at night.

Fearsome fangs
The gaboon viper is an extremely poisonous snake. It may contain enough venom to kill 20 people. Its fangs are up to 2 inches long and enable it to inject poisonous venom deep into the bodies of the small animals and birds it hunts. The patterns on the viper's skin act as camouflage.

Okapi
(*Okapia johnstoni*)
Length: up to 6 ft 6 in
Height at shoulder:
5 ft 6 in

Gaboon viper
(*Bitis gabonica*)
Length: up to 6 ft 6 in

Striped legs
The stripes on the okapi's legs help to break up the outline of its body when it is standing among the trees. This hides it from predators, such as the leopard. The okapi feeds on leaves, which it pulls from trees and bushes with its tongue. Its tongue is so long that the okapi can use it to clean its eyes and eyelids. The okapi's closest relation is the giraffe. The male okapi has short, fur-covered horns, like a giraffe's.

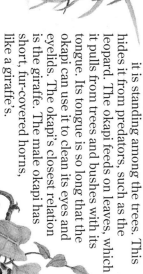

Powerful hunter
The leopard is so strong that it can drag the dead body of an animal weighing almost as much as itself. It stores large items of food in the branches of a tree to keep other animals from stealing its meals. The leopard's prey includes antelopes, monkeys, birds, fishes, and snakes. Unlike most other cats, the mother leopard does not teach her cubs how to hunt. They have to learn how to fend for themselves and are not able to survive without their mother until they are 18 months to two years old.

Leopard
(*Panthera pardus*)
Body length: up to 6 ft 3 in
Tail: up to 4 ft 6 in

Black-casqued hornbill
(*Ceratogymna atrata*)
Length: up to
2 ft 8 in
Female: 2 ft 6 in

Noisy feathers

As the black-casqued hornbill flies through the rainforest, its broad wings make a loud swishing noise. This is caused by air rushing through gaps between its flight feathers. The strange horny ridge along the top of its bill is called a casque. The bird probably recognizes the age, sex, and species of other hornbills from their casques.

Hippopotamus
(*Hippopotamus amphibius*)
Length: up to 14 ft 9 in
Height at shoulder: 5 ft

Open wide

Hippopotamuses often fight each other. A hippo threatens a rival by opening its mouth wide to show off its long, fearsome teeth. This is caused by air rushing resting in lakes and rivers or on sand banks. It comes out at night to munch the grass on lake shores and river banks. A hippo can eat up to 180 pounds of grass and other plant material in one night. The hippopotamus has webbed toes which help it to swim. It can stay underwater for up to six minutes.

Goliath frog
(*Gigantorana goliath*)
Length: up to 12 in

Giant leaper

The goliath frog has long back legs and can travel more than 10 feet in one leap. Its short front legs help to absorb the impact of landing. Its giant leaps help this huge frog to escape from enemies. Like all frogs, the goliath frog is a strong swimmer. It propels itself through the water with its back legs and webbed feet.

African jacana
(*Actophilornis africanus*)
Length: up to 11 in

Water walker

The African jacana's long toes help to spread its weight and enable it to walk over floating water plants, such as lilies. It is sometimes called the lilytrotter. As it stalks over the vegetation, it snaps up water insects and shellfish in its pointed bill. The African jacana sometimes hides from predators by sinking under the water, leaving only its bill and nostrils showing.

Chimpanzee
(*Pan troglodytes*)
Height: up to
3 ft 1 in

Tool user

The chimpanzee is extremely intelligent and is one of the few animals known to make and use tools. It can break off a twig, poke it into a termite nest, and pull it out crawling with tasty termites. It can use a stone as a hammer. The chimpanzee is equally at home in the trees and on the ground. It walks on all fours, with its fingers curled up to take its weight on its knuckles. At night, the chimpanzee builds a nest of twigs and branches to sleep in.

Super snail

The giant African snail eats all kinds of plants. It uses its rough tongue to scrape pieces from the plant. At the end of its long tentacles, the snail has simple eyes that can only tell light from dark. It uses the shorter tentacles on its head for smelling and feeling things.

Giant African snail
(*Achatina fulica*)
Length: up to 13 in

In places the walls of the Great Rift Valley are 4,000 feet high.

Much of the African rainforest lies in the basin of the Zaire River.

Huge flocks of flamingos live on the lakes in the Great Rift Valley.

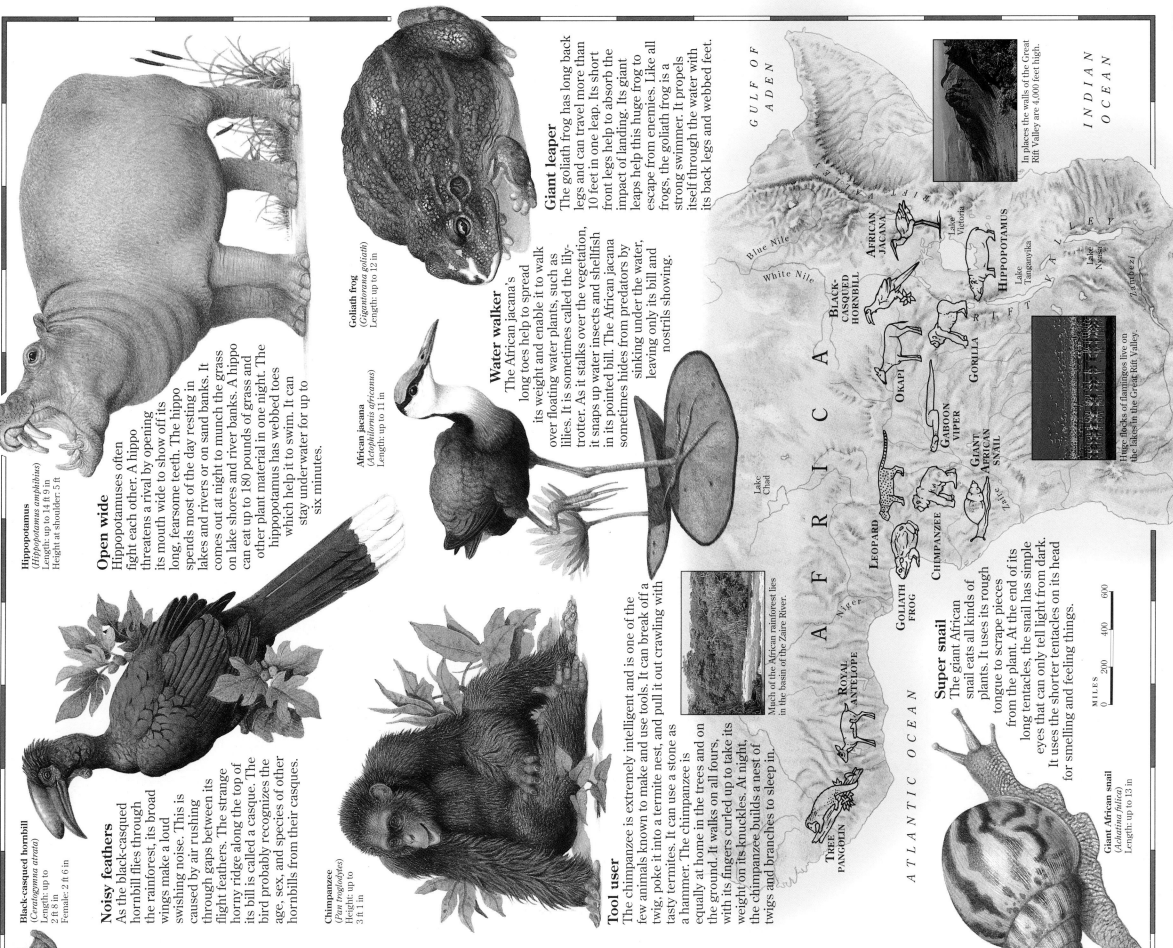

GULF OF ADEN

INDIAN OCEAN

ATLANTIC OCEAN

RIFT VALLEY

A F R I C A

Blue Nile

White Nile

Lake Chad

Niger

Lake Victoria

Lake Tanganyika

Lake Nyasa

Zambezi

Zaire

AFRICAN JACANA

BLACK-CASQUED HORNBILL

HIPPOPOTAMUS

OKAPI

GORILLA

GABOON VIPER

GIANT AFRICAN SNAIL

LEOPARD

CHIMPANZEE

GOLIATH FROG

ROYAL ANTELOPE

TREE PANGOLIN

MILES
0   200   400   600

The Savanna

THE SWEEPING GRASSLANDS of the African savanna are almost the last place on Earth where spectacular herds of large grazing animals survive. There are two main seasons, wet and dry. At the start of the dry season huge herds gather together and make long journeys to find fresh grass and water. The migrating herds sometimes fill the plains as far as the eye can see.

Most of the grazing animals feed on grasses, but each species eats a different part of the grass, so they seldom compete for food. Zebras eat the tough tops of the grass stems, wildebeest eat the leafy center, and gazelles prefer the young shoots close to the ground. The plant eaters themselves are a source of food for the hunters of the savanna – lions, leopards, cheetahs, and wild dogs. After a kill, vultures and other scavengers move in and clean up the leftovers. In the grasses at the feet of the larger animals live lizards, snakes, and millions of insects, which all play a vital role in the life of the grasslands.

Super soldier
The soldier termite defends its colony by using its head and strong jaws to stab and wound attackers.

Soldier termite
(*Bellicositermes natalensis*)
Length: up to 1 in

Giant eaters
African elephants spend up to 16 hours a day searching for enough food to support their massive bodies. A big male can weigh as much as 90 adult humans. Elephants use their long trunks to reach leaves and shoots high on the trees. They are strong enough to push over trees to reach the new leaves on the top branches. Each elephant uses one tusk more than the other; in the same way that people are right- or left-handed.

African elephant
(*Loxodonta africana*)
Height at shoulder:
up to 11 ft 8 in
Trunk: up to 7 ft

Blue wildebeest
(*Connochaetes taurinus*)
Height at shoulder: 4 ft 6 in
Body length: 7 ft

Group protection
Zebras usually live in family groups, but in the dry season they gather in large herds. This helps to protect them against predators, since many pairs of eyes and ears are more likely to spot danger. Zebra stallions sometimes kick out at predators, such as lions, and may smash their teeth.

Burchell's zebra
(*Equus burchelli*)
Height at shoulder: 4 ft
Body length: up to 8 ft

Lightning cat
The cheetah relies on short bursts of incredible speed to catch its prey. It can sprint at more than 62 mph over short distances, but tires easily. It grips the throat of its prey with its long, pointed canine teeth. Its razor-sharp back teeth slice meat off the bones.

Cheetah
(*Acinonyx jubatus*)
Body length:
7 ft 6 in
Tail: 2 ft 6 in

Tireless trekker
Wildebeest trek thousands of miles across the savanna searching for fresh grass. Whenever they stop to rest or graze, each male stakes out a territory which he guards against other males. Baby wildebeest can run soon after they are born, and in a few hours they are able to keep up with the rest of the herd.

Bone cruncher
Hyenas have massive jaws that are strong enough to crunch through bones. They hunt in small groups at night, killing animals such as wildebeest and zebra by disemboweling them. They also eat animals killed by other predators.

Spotted hyena (*Crocuta crocuta*)
Height at shoulder: 3 ft
Body length: up to 5 ft 4 in

ATLANTIC OCEAN

Zaire

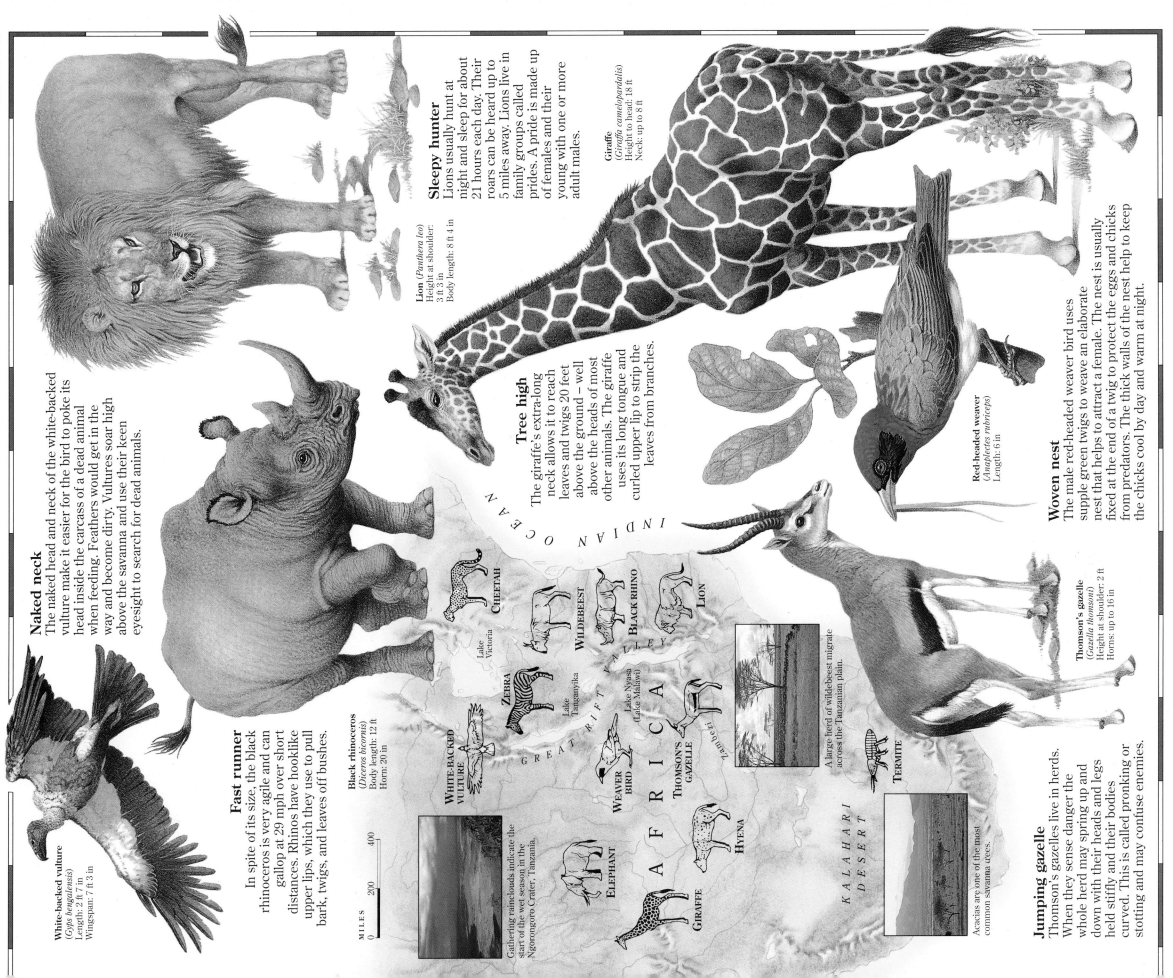

Sleepy hunter

Lions usually hunt at night and sleep for about 21 hours each day. Their roars can be heard up to 5 miles away. Lions live in family groups called prides. A pride is made up of females and their young with one or more adult males.

Lion (*Panthera leo*)
Height at shoulder:
3 ft 3 in
Body length: 8 ft 4 in

Giraffe
(*Giraffa camelopardalis*)
Height to head: 18 ft
Neck: up to 8 ft

Tree high

The giraffe's extra-long neck allows it to reach leaves and twigs 20 feet above the ground – well above the heads of most other animals. The giraffe uses its long tongue and curled upper lip to strip the leaves from branches.

Woven nest

The male red-headed weaver bird uses supple green twigs to weave an elaborate nest that helps to attract a female. The nest is usually fixed at the end of a twig to protect the eggs and chicks from predators. The thick walls of the nest help to keep the chicks cool by day and warm at night.

Red-headed weaver
(*Anaplectes rubriceps*)
Length: 6 in

Naked neck

The naked head and neck of the white-backed vulture make it easier for the bird to poke its head inside the carcass of a dead animal when feeding. Feathers would get in the way and become dirty. Vultures soar high above the savanna and use their keen eyesight to search for dead animals.

White-backed vulture
(*Gyps bengalensis*)
Length: 2 ft 7 in
Wingspan: 7 ft 3 in

Fast runner

In spite of its size, the black rhinoceros is very agile and can gallop at 29 mph over short distances. Rhinos have hooklike upper lips, which they use to pull bark, twigs, and leaves off bushes.

Black rhinoceros
(*Diceros bicornis*)
Body length: 12 ft
Horn: 20 in

Jumping gazelle

Thomson's gazelles live in herds. When they sense danger the whole herd may spring up and down with their heads and legs held stiffly and their bodies curved. This is called pronking or stotting and may confuse enemies.

Thomson's gazelle
(*Gazella thomsoni*)
Height at shoulder: 2 ft
Horns: up to 16 in

MILES
0   200   400

Gathering rainclouds indicate the start of the wet season in the Ngorongoro Crater, Tanzania.

A large herd of wildebeest migrate across the Tanzanian plain.

Acacias are one of the most common savanna trees.

INDIAN OCEAN

GREAT RIFT VALLEY

AFRICA

KALAHARI DESERT

Lake Victoria
Lake Tanganyika
Lake Nyasa (Lake Malawi)
Zambezi

CHEETAH
WILDEBEEST
BLACK RHINO
LION
ZEBRA
THOMSON'S GAZELLE
WHITE-BACKED VULTURE
WEAVER BIRD
HYENA
ELEPHANT
GIRAFFE
TERMITE

Madagascar

MADAGASCAR is the fourth largest island in the world. It was once attached to mainland Africa, but it split off and drifted away tens of millions of years ago. The long period of isolation has allowed many unique animals to develop there. These include tenrecs, lemurs, the fossa, and two-thirds of the world's chameleons. In contrast, some common groups of animals do not occur on the island at all. There are no woodpeckers, for example, and no poisonous snakes.

One of the reasons for the wide range of wildlife on Madagascar is the varied climate and vegetation of the island. On the east coast is an area of tropical rainforest. The extreme south of the island is much drier, with semi-desert conditions. A backbone of mountains runs from north to south down the island, while the high central plateau is relatively cold and is covered with grassy savannah.

Ring-tailed lemur
(*Lemur catta*)
Body length: 18 in
Tail: 22 in

Smelly signals

The ring-tailed lemur has three kinds of scent gland which it uses to mark its territory. These smelly signals tell rival lemurs to keep out. The male ring-tail also uses his scent in "stink fights" with other males. He spreads scent over his tail from the glands on his wrists and armpits. Then he shakes his tail over his back to fan the smell toward the rival. Males may battle like this for as long as an hour. Lemurs live in troops of up to 40 members. They feed on fruit, leaves, tree bark, and grass.

Clever climber

The fossa's tail is almost as long as its body and helps it to balance when climbing trees. The fossa's prey include lemurs and other mammals, birds, reptiles, and insects, which it catches and holds with a bite on the back of the head. The fossa is the most widespread meat-eating animal on Madagascar. It has been able to thrive there because there are no cats or dogs on the island, so it faces little competition.

Fossa
(*Cryptoprocta ferox*)
Body length: up to 2 ft 5 in
Tail: up to 2 ft 3 in

Sugar straw

The false sunbird uses its long, curved beak to reach the sweet nectar hidden deep inside flowers. The sides of its tongue curl up to form a straw through which it sucks up the nectar. As it feeds, the sunbird carries pollen from one flower to another and helps to pollinate the plants. In the breeding season, the male sunbird develops bare blue skin on the sides of his head. This probably attracts females for mating.

False sunbird
(*Neodrepanis coruscans*)
Length: 4 in

Strange call

The sifaka's name comes from the strange call it makes to warn other sifakas of danger – "shi-fakh! shi-fakh!" The sifaka spends the day resting in the treetops. Holding its arms wide, it sunbathes in the morning to warm up after the cold night. Its legs are longer than its arms and enable it to leap more than 30 feet through the trees. Occasionally, the sifaka comes down to the ground and hops along on its back legs, waving its arms wildly over its head. Its arms are too short to enable it to run on all fours.

Sifaka
(*Propithecus verreauxi*)
Body length: 18 in
Tail: 21 in

Largest litter

The female tailless tenrec produces the largest litter of any mammal – up to 32 young at one time. Only about 16 to 20 usually survive. The tailless tenrec has a coat of stiff hairs and spines. To frighten predators away, the tenrec raises the spines and hair on its head and back, stamps its front feet, opens its mouth wide, and hisses.

Tailless tenrec
(*Tenrec ecaudatus*)
Length: up to 15 in

Outsize ears

The aye-aye is a type of lemur. It has huge, batlike ears, and its hearing is so good that it can detect insects moving beneath the bark of a tree. It uses its long, spindly middle finger to pull out juicy grubs. The aye-aye also eats nuts, bamboo shoots, and fruit. It lives in forests and spends most of its time in the trees. The aye-aye is now on the verge of extinction because its habitat is being destroyed.

Aye-aye
(*Daubentonia madagascariensis*)
Body length: 18 in
Tail: 22 in

MILES
0   50   100   150

Stick insect
(*Stipleidea sipylus*)
Length: 3.5 in

A plain about 30 miles wide lies along the eastern coast of Madagascar.

Twiggy body
There are about 80 different kinds of stick insect on Madagascar, and none of these are found anywhere else in the world. The long, thin bodies of stick insects look so much like twigs that they are almost impossible to spot, especially since they can stay very still.

INDIAN OCEAN

TSARATANANA MASSIF

AVE-AYE

PARSON'S CHAMELEON

CORAL-BILLED NUTHATCH VANGA

FOSSA

FALSE SUNBIRD

INDRI

Betsiboka

BUSH PIG

CENTRAL PLATEAU

MADAGASCAR

Mania

TAILLESS TENREC

SIFAKA

RING-TAILED LEMUR

STICK INSECT

Mangoky

Onilahy

MOZAMBIQUE CHANNEL

Parson's chameleon
(*Chamaeleo parsoni*)
Length: 16 in

Pincer toes
Parson's chameleon has hands and feet like pincers, with two toes opposite the other three. This allows it to get a firm grip on branches and plants. Chameleons can change color according to their mood (when they are angry or frightened, for example) or to match their surroundings. This camouflages them from predators and helps them to creep up on their prey without being seen.

Much of Madagascar was once covered by forest. The few forests that remain are home to a huge variety of plants and animals.

Noisy lemur
The indri is the largest of the lemurs and makes the most noise. Its loud wails can be heard 2 miles away, and if a family of indris calls together the sound is deafening. These calls help to keep rival groups away. Each indri can probably identify the individuals in other groups by their cries. When an indri is alarmed, it makes a different, hooting call.

COELACANTH

Grasses are the main form of vegetation on the central plateau of Madagascar.

Indri
(*Indri indri*)
Body length: up to 2 ft 3 in
Tail: up to 2 in

Probing bill
The coral-billed nuthatch vanga feeds on insects. It lives in the humid rainforests of eastern Madagascar, where it clings to tree trunks with its sharp claws and probes the bark for insect grubs with its bill. It belongs to a group of birds called the vanga shrikes, which live only on Madagascar.

Coral-billed nuthatch vanga
(*Hypositta corallirostris*)
Length: up to 5 in

Living fossil
Scientists believed the coelacanth had died out 70 million years ago until a living fish was caught off the coast of Madagascar in 1938. The coelacanth may look like the first fishes that crawled out of the water onto land millions of years ago. Over many years, some of these fishes developed into amphibians, like the modern frog and newt. Like those early fishes, the coelacanth has limb-like fins, which probably help it to move over the rocky seafloor.

Coelacanth
(*Latimeria chalumnae*)
Length: up to 6 ft 2 in

Hairy back
The bush pig, a wild boar, has a mane of long, whitish hairs along its back. It raises its mane when it is excited or alarmed. The bush pig uses its long, sensitive snout to sniff out roots, insects, and worms but will eat almost anything, from plant material to small mammals, birds, and dead animals. Bush pigs cause damage to crops and are often hunted by farmers.

Bush pig
(*Potamochoerus porcus*)
Body length: up to 5 ft
Tail: up to 18 in

Siberia

THE CONIFER FORESTS OF SIBERIA in northern Asia make up the largest area of forest in the world. The most common trees are larch, fir, and spruce. Their cones provide a vital source of food for animals, especially during the snowy winter months. South of the forests lies Lake Baikal. This lake has been isolated for millions of years, and many of the animals that live there are not found anywhere else in the world.

To the north of the forest belt are the vast Arctic wastelands, called the tundra, where the ground is frozen for much of the year. During the winter, which lasts for nine months of the year, many animals move south to the shelter of the conifer forests and birds fly away to warmer climates. The brief tundra summer is a time of plenty, when it is light for 24 hours a day.

Whooper swan
(*Cygnus cygnus*)
Length: 4 ft 10 in
Wingspan: 5 ft

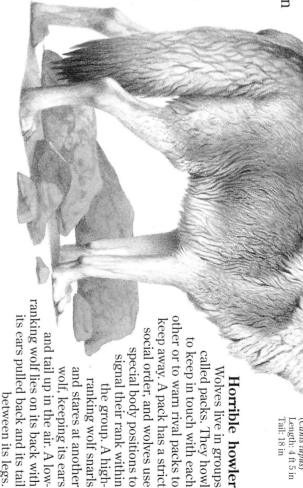

Trumpet call
The whooper swan is one of the noisiest swans in the world. It gets its name from its loud, trumpeting call, which can be heard over great distances. Its wings make a swishing sound when it flies. Whooper swans often gather together in flocks of hundreds. They breed in the tundra regions and on lakes deep in the conifer forests.

Unique seal
The Baikal seal is the only seal that lives in fresh water. It is related to the ringed seals that live in the Arctic Ocean. Millions of years ago, its ancestors probably swam from the Arctic up the Lena River to reach Lake Baikal. Now the seal cannot escape from the waters of the lake. The Baikal seal feeds on fish, snapping them up with its sharp teeth.

Baikal seal
(*Phoca sibirica*)
Length: up to 5 ft

Sealing wax
The waxwing is named for the red dots on its wings. They look like drops of the wax that people once used to seal letters. No one knows what these markings are for. The waxwing feeds mainly on berries and digests its food very quickly. Seeds can pass through its digestive system in as little as 16 minutes.

Waxwing
(*Bombycilla garrulus*)
Length: 7 in

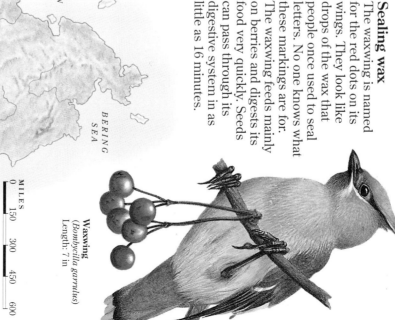

Horrible howler
Wolves live in groups called packs. They howl to keep in touch with each other or to warn rival packs to keep away. A pack has a strict social order, and wolves use special body positions to signal their rank within the group. A high-ranking wolf snarls and stares at another wolf, keeping its ears and tail up in the air. A low-ranking wolf lies on its back with its ears pulled back and its tail between its legs.

Wolf
(*Canis lupus*)
Length: 4 ft 5 in
Tail: 18 in

Map labels

BARENTS SEA

NOVAYA ZEMLYA

KARA SEA

SEVERNAYA ZEMLYA

LAPTEV SEA

NOVOSIBIRSKIYE OSTROVA

EAST SIBERIAN SEA

ARCTIC OCEAN

U R A L   M T S

Ob

Yenisei

Angara

Lena

Lena

Indirka

S   I   B   E   R   I   A

Lake Baikal

SEA OF OKHOTSK

BERING SEA

KAMCHATKA PENINSULA

S A K H A L I N

SIBERIAN TIT

HAZEL GROUSE

SABLE

REINDEER

WOLF

WAXWING

SNOWY OWL

SIBERIAN LEMMING

ARCTIC GROUND SQUIRREL

SIBERIAN JAY

WHOOPER SWAN

BAIKAL SEAL

The huge expanses of Siberian forests cover one-fourth of the world's forested areas.

Lake Baikal is the deepest and oldest lake on Earth. It also contains more water than any other lake.

MILES
0
150
300
450
600

Reindeer
(*Rangifer tarandus*)
Body length:
up to 7 ft 2 in
Tail: up to 8 in

Snowshoe hooves

The reindeer, or caribou, has broad hooves that enable it to walk easily in deep snow. In winter, the reindeer uses its hooves to scrape away the snow so that it can feed on the lichens and mosses underneath. Some reindeer migrate between their summer breeding grounds on the tundra and their winter feeding grounds in the conifer forests. Reindeer are the only deer in which both the male and the female have antlers.

Speckled feathers

The brown, speckled markings on the feathers of the female hazel grouse serve to hide her from predators while she is sitting on her eggs. The hazel grouse has large flight muscles, which also store food and can be used to produce heat if the grouse gets very cold. Grouse are the most common and widespread birds in the conifer forests.

Siberian tit
(*Parus cinctus*)
Length: 5 in

Energy saver

The Siberian tit stays in the forests all year round, despite the freezing winter temperatures. At night, its heartbeat and other body processes slow down, and its temperature drops so that it uses up less energy. This helps it to survive when energy-giving food is hard to find. The tit uses its short, sturdy bill to pluck insects, seeds, and berries from the trees and bushes.

Moving house

Every three or four years, the number of lemmings increases so much that thousands leave their nests to look for new homes. Once on the move, lemmings will not stop, even in large towns or at busy crossroads. Many are eaten by predators or die from exhaustion or starvation. Others drown trying to cross rivers, lakes, or the sea, but they do not commit suicide, as many people believe.

Hazel grouse
(*Bonasa bonasia*)
Length: 14 in

Fur coat

The sable was hunted almost to extinction for its thick, beautiful coat. Some sables are now specially bred on fur farms; and others have been reared in captivity and released back into the wild, so the sable is no longer an endangered species. The sable feeds on small mammals, such as voles, as well as fish, insects, nuts, and berries. It has well-developed scent glands and uses this scent to mark the edges of its territory. These scent marks act as smelly messages to other sables to keep away.

Powerful hunter

The huge and powerful snowy owl glides silently over the frozen tundra in search of lemmings and voles. It can catch up to 10 lemmings in one day and is strong enough to catch and kill hares. The snowy owl's white or white-and-black speckled plumage camouflages it against the snow. The thick feathers on its legs, which look like long socks, help to keep it warm.

Snowy owl
(*Nyctea scandiaca*)
Length: up to
2 ft 2 in
Wingspan: up to
5 ft 2 in

Siberian lemming
(*Lemmus sibiricus*)
Length: up to 7 in

Underground larders

The Arctic ground squirrel stores food in its underground burrow during the short summer season. It makes several "larders" of food to last through its winter sleep, or hibernation. It also eats a lot in the summer to build up stores of fat in its body. If the ground squirrel is frightened by a hawk above, it gives a shrill whistle that warns other ground squirrels.

Arctic ground squirrel
(*Spermophilus parryi*)
Body: up to 14 in
Tail: up to 6 in

Sable (*Martes zibellina*)
Body length: up to 18 in
Tail: up to 7 in

Siberian jay
(*Perisoreus infaustus*)
Length: 11 in

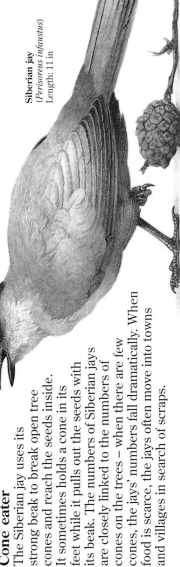

Cone eater

The Siberian jay uses its strong beak to break open tree cones and reach the seeds inside. It sometimes holds a cone in its feet while it pulls out the seeds with its beak. The numbers of Siberian jays are closely linked to the numbers of cones on the trees – when there are few cones, the jays' numbers fall dramatically. When food is scarce, the jays often move into towns and villages in search of scraps.

Deserts and Steppes

A VAST AREA OF GRASSLAND called the steppes stretches across the southern part of the USSR and into China. The climate in this region consists of very hot summers and long, icy winters with cold winds blowing down from the frozen north. The steppes were once populated by huge herds of grazing animals, such as saigas and onagers, but they have been almost wiped out by hunting. Some of the remaining herds are now protected, but they are forced to live in drier areas, away from farms. The most common animals on the steppes are burrowing rodents, such as the suslik.

South of the steppes lie the deserts of central Asia, where rainfall is less than 12 inches a year. Summers are baking hot, but at night the temperature can drop by as much as 36° F. Some desert animals sleep through the summer months; others come out only at night to escape the heat of the day. Small animals, such as the jerboa, are adapted to survive without drinking. Some larger animals, such as the camel, store fat in their bodies to keep them going when food and water are scarce.

Common hamster
(*Cricetus cricetus*)
Body length: up to 12 in
Tail: up to 2 in

Cheek pouches
The hamster feeds on seeds, grain, roots, plants, and insects. In late summer, it stores large supplies of food in a network of tunnels that it digs beneath the steppe, carrying the food to its burrow in special cheek pouches. Hamsters have been known to store as much as 2 pounds of food. During the winter, the hamster hibernates in its burrow, waking every so often for a snack.

Lethal viper
The levantine viper is one of the largest of the desert snakes. It is poisonous and kills by injecting venom into its prey through its long, hollow fangs. It waits in a concealed position to ambush and strike the rodents and lizards on which it feeds. The viper waits for its victim to die and then swallows it whole. It rests in the shade or below ground during the heat of the day, coming out only at night to hunt.

Levantine viper
(*Vipera lebetina*)
Length: up to 6 ft

Rare eagle
The rare steppe eagle nests on the ground because there are so few trees on the open steppe grasslands. It is a fierce hunter, especially of small rodents such as hamsters, lemmings, susliks, and marmots. The eagle swoops down from the sky and seizes its prey with its strong, sharp talons. Then, with its hooked beak, it tears its food into bite-sized pieces.

Steppe eagle
(*Aquila nipalensis*)
Length: up to 2 ft 10 in
Wingspan: up to 5 ft 9 in

Monitor lizard
Monitor lizard
(*Varanus griseus*)
Length: up to 5 ft

Huge lizard
The giant monitor lizard eats almost anything, from other lizards and tortoises to rodents and birds. Sometimes it even eats its own young. It swallows its prey whole, like a snake. To frighten enemies away, the monitor lizard hisses loudly and lashes its powerful tail from side to side. It may also bite. Monitor lizards are becoming rare because people kill them for their skins.

Onager
(*Equus hemionus*)
Length: 6 ft 6 in
Height at shoulder:
up to 4 ft 7 in

Fast runner
The onager, or wild ass, can run at speeds of 40 mph or more, as fast as any race horse. It can go for two or three days without drinking, which helps it to survive in the dry conditions of the deserts and steppes. In summer the onager lives on the high grassland; in winter it migrates to lower levels to find water and fresh grass to eat.

One hump or two?
The bactrian camel of central Asia has two humps. The Arabian camel has only one. Most bactrian camels have been domesticated, but a small number of them still live wild in the Gobi Desert. The bactrian can survive in very high and very low temperatures. In winter it grows long, shaggy hair which keeps it warm; in the summer most of this hair falls out. The bactrian has wide, flat feet that enable it to walk over the soft sand without sinking in.

Bactrian camel
(*Camelus bactrianus*)
Body length:
up to 9 ft 9 in
Height at shoulder:
up to 6 ft 6 in

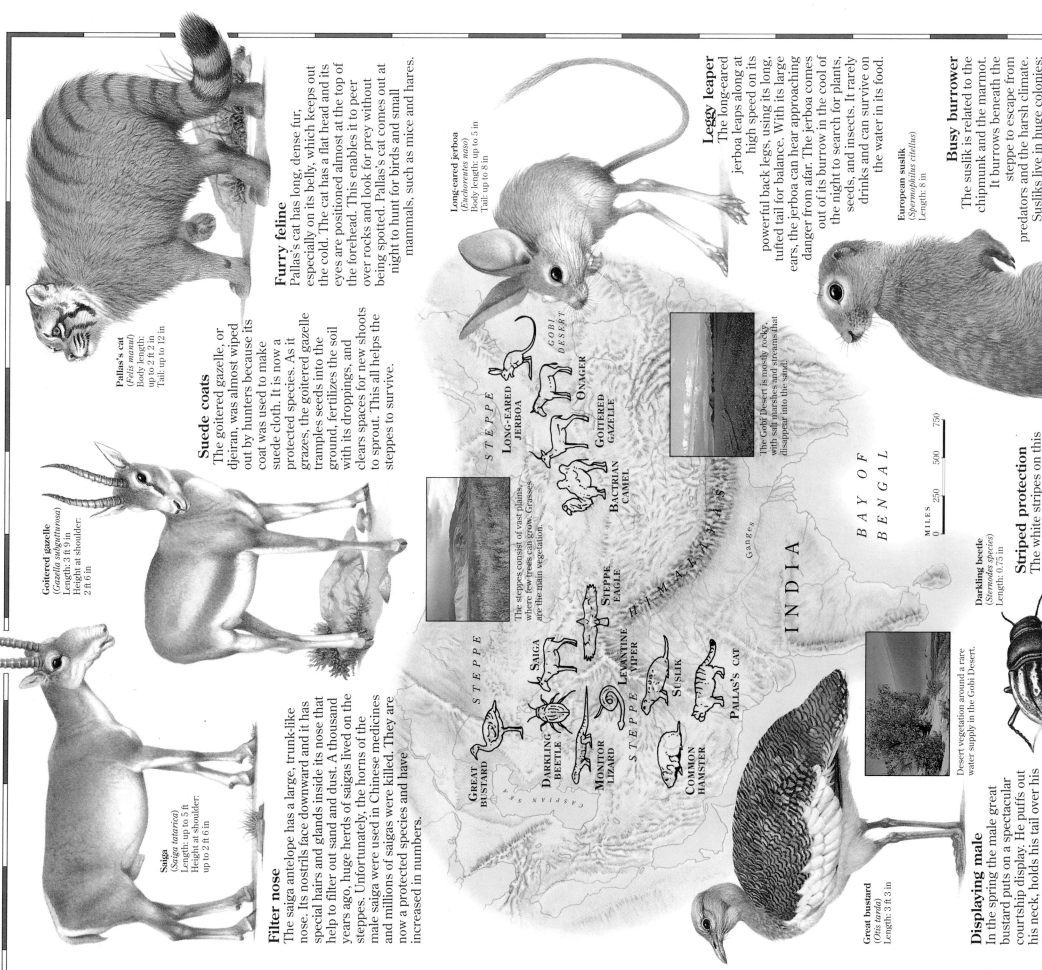

Pallas's cat
(*Felis manul*)
Body length:
up to 2 ft 2 in
Tail: up to 12 in

Furry feline
Pallas's cat has long, dense fur, especially on its belly, which keeps out the cold. The cat has a flat head and its eyes are positioned almost at the top of the forehead. This enables it to peer over rocks and look for prey without being spotted. Pallas's cat comes out at night to hunt for birds and small mammals, such as mice and hares.

Suede coats
The goitered gazelle, or djeiran, was almost wiped out by hunters because its coat was used to make suede cloth. It is now a protected species. As it grazes, the goitered gazelle tramples seeds into the ground, fertilizes the soil with its droppings, and clears spaces for new shoots to sprout. This all helps the steppes to survive.

Goitered gazelle
(*Gazella subgutturosa*)
Length: 3 ft 9 in
Height at shoulder:
2 ft 6 in

Saiga
(*Saiga tatarica*)
Length: up to 5 ft
Height at shoulder:
up to 2 ft 6 in

Filter nose
The saiga antelope has a large, trunk-like nose. Its nostrils face downward and it has special hairs and glands inside its nose that help to filter out sand and dust. A thousand years ago, huge herds of saigas lived on the steppes. Unfortunately, the horns of the male saiga were used in Chinese medicines and millions of saigas were killed. They are now a protected species and have increased in numbers.

Long-eared jerboa
(*Euchoreutes naso*)
Body length: up to 5 in
Tail: up to 8 in

Leggy leaper
The long-eared jerboa leaps along at high speed on its powerful back legs, using its long, tufted tail for balance. With its large ears, the jerboa can hear approaching danger from afar. The jerboa comes out of its burrow in the cool of the night to search for plants, seeds, and insects. It rarely drinks and can survive on the water in its food.

European suslik
(*Spermophilus citellus*)
Length: 8 in

Busy burrower
The suslik is related to the chipmunk and the marmot. It burrows beneath the steppe to escape from predators and the harsh climate. Susliks live in huge colonies; there may be up to 12,000 burrows in a field the size of a basketball court. Their digging churns up the ground and brings fresh soil to the surface. Their droppings also enrich the soil and help the grasses to grow.

The Gobi Desert is mostly rocky, with salt marshes and streams that disappear into the sand.

The steppes consist of vast plains, where few trees can grow. Grasses are the main vegetation.

MILES
0 250 500 750

GOBI DESERT

STEPPE

LONG-EARED JERBOA
ONAGER
GOITERED GAZELLE
BACTRIAN CAMEL
STEPPE EAGLE
SAIGA
LEVANTINE VIPER
SUSLIK
PALLAS'S CAT
GREAT BUSTARD
DARKLING BEETLE
MONITOR LIZARD
COMMON HAMSTER

H I M A L A Y A S

Ganges

INDIA

BAY OF BENGAL

CASPIAN SEA

STEPPE

Desert vegetation around a rare water supply in the Gobi Desert.

Striped protection
The white stripes on this darkling beetle break up the outline of its body. This provides camouflage, and predators cannot see the beetle against the sand. The thick shell and compact shape of the darkling beetle reduce water loss and help the insect survive the heat of the desert.

Darkling beetle
(*Sternodes species*)
Length: 0.75 in

Great bustard
(*Otis tarda*)
Length: 3 ft 3 in

Displaying male
In the spring the male great bustard puts on a spectacular courtship display. He puffs out his neck, holds his tail over his back, and spreads his wings to form two huge, white rosettes on the sides of his body. The great bustard is one of the largest flying birds, although it usually walks or runs. The name "bustard" means "the bird that walks."

The Himalayas

THE HIMALAYAS are a gigantic chain of mountains that stretch across northern India for a distance of about 1,500 miles. Among the mountains are many of the highest mountains in the world; snow and ice cover many of the peaks all year round. The mountain chain separates the cool Asian lands to the north from the tropical regions of northern India. There is a wide variety of habitats in the Himalayas – tropical forests in the foothills, rhododendron and bamboo forests and grassy meadows higher up, bleak tundra areas below the peaks.

Only insects can survive at the high altitudes of the mountain peaks. They feed on plant spores, pollen, and other insects, all of which are swept up from the Indian plains by the strong winds. Most animals live farther down the slopes in the forests and meadows. The mountain animals have thick fur and large lungs to help them survive the cold, the wind, and the thin air. Many animals, such as snow leopards and ibexes, move down to the snow-free lower slopes and valleys in winter. Others, such as marmots and bears, hibernate during the coldest months.

Blood pheasant
(*Ithaginis cruentus*)
Length: 18 in

Huge horns

The male Siberian ibex has huge horns which he uses in spectacular "head-butting" contests with rival males. The female bird has dowdy brown feathers that camouflage her while she is sitting on her eggs. Blood pheasants make their nests in grass-lined gaps between large boulders. They eat pine shoots, mosses, ferns, and lichens.

Red stripes

The blood pheasant gets its name from the red stripes on the male's feathers. These bright colors help him to attract a female for mating.

The male Siberian ibex has huge horns which he uses in spectacular "head-butting" contests with rival enemies. It migrates to the lower slopes in winter, and its thick coat helps it to survive the harsh winter months. The ibex can leap nimbly among the rocky crags where it is safe from most

Siberian ibex
(*Capra ibex sibirica*)
Height at shoulder:
3 ft 3 in

The grassy meadows on the lower mountain slopes provide food for many grazing animals.

Mount Everest, the highest mountain in the world, is one of the Himalayan peaks.

High hunter

The powerful snow leopard, or ounce, feeds on wild sheep and goats, which it hunts up to 18,000 feet up in the mountains. In winter, it follows its prey down into the forests. The snow leopard can make huge leaps over ravines. Its long, thick fur keeps it warm, and its broad feet stop it from sinking into the snow. Adult snow leopards usually live alone, roaming around their huge territories.

Bhutan glory (*Bhutanitis lidderdale*)
Wingspan: up to 4.5 in

Graceful leaper

The Hanuman langur is a graceful monkey that can leap up to 30 feet through the trees. Its long tail helps it to balance. The langur feeds on young leaves, fruit, and flowers, and it has a complex stomach and ridged teeth to help it digest its tough food. It is named after Hanuman, the Hindu monkey god, and is a sacred animal in India.

Flashy colors

When it rests, the Bhutan glory folds its front wings over its back wings to hide the colorful markings. If it is disturbed by a predator, it suddenly reveals these bright colors. This may confuse the predator and allow the butterfly time to escape. Markings such as these are called "flash colors." The Bhutan glory flies at altitudes of 5,000 to 9,000 feet in the Himalayan forests.

Hanuman langur
(*Presbytis entellus*)
Body length: up to 3 ft 3 in
Tail: up to 3 ft 3 in

Snow leopard
(*Panthera uncia*)
Body length:
up to 5 ft
Tail: 3 ft

Indus

Sutlej

Indus

Ganges

I N D I A

H
I
M
A
L
A
Y
A

BOBAK MARMOT
HANUMAN LANGUR
HIMALAYAN BLACK BEAR
TAKIN
MARKHOR
WILD YAK

HIMALAYAN GRIFFON VULTURE
BLOOD PHEASANT
SIBERIAN IBEX

MILES
0
100
200
300

Corkscrew head

The markhor is a wild goat. It has huge spiral horns that may grow up to 4 feet long. Both male and female animals have horns, but the female's horns are smaller. The markhor's coat is short and smooth in summer and grows longer in winter to keep out the cold. The markhor moves down the mountains to find warmer places in winter. The markhor is nearly extinct because of hunting and because of diseases caught from domestic animals.

Markhor
(*Capra falconeri*)
Body length: up to 5 ft 2 in
Tail: up to 5.5 in

Fire bird

The fire-tailed myzornis has red markings on its wings and tail, making the bird look as if it is on fire. The female's red markings are duller than those of the male. This tiny bird lives in the evergreen mountain forests of Nepal. It feeds on tree sap and nectar, which it laps up with its bristly tongue.

Fire-tailed myzornis
(*Myzornis pyrrhoura*)
Length: 5 in

Takin
(*Budorcas taxicolor*)
Body length: 4 ft
Tail: 4 in

Winter sleep

The bobak marmot sleeps through the cold winter months in the warmth and safety of its burrow. Marmots live in groups, and one animal always stands guard to warn the others of any danger. Marmots feed on plants. They come out in the early morning to search for food.

Bobak marmot
(*Marmota bobak*)
Body length: 2 ft
Tail: up to 6 in

Sturdy legs

The takin has thick, strong legs and large hooves, which enable it to climb the steep slopes, and a dense coat that keeps it warm. In summer, large herds of takin live high up on the mountains in dense rhododendron and bamboo thickets. In winter, they move down to the valleys. Young takin can follow their mothers over the slopes when they are only three days old.

Himalayan black bear
(*Selenarctos thibetanus*)
Length: 5 ft 7 in
Height at shoulder: 3 ft

Snoozing bear

In winter, when food is hard to find, the Himalayan black bear hibernates in a cave or tree hole. It eats as much as possible in the autumn to build up fat reserves in its body. This fat keeps it alive during the winter months. The Himalayan black bear lives in the forests on the lower slopes of the mountains. It can climb well and is a good swimmer. Sometimes it curls into a ball and rolls downhill.

Himalayan griffon vulture
(*Gyps himalayensis*)
Wingspan: 4 ft 2 in

Furry fringe

The wild yak has a long, furry coat which reaches almost to the ground. Under the long hairs is a layer of short, dense underfur that insulates the yak from the freezing winter temperatures. In spring, the yak molts this underfur and looks very ragged. The wild yak is nimble and sure-footed, despite its huge size. It has been hunted almost to extinction and now lives only in remote places at altitudes of about 15,000 feet.

Wild yak (*Bos mutus*)
Length: 9 ft 9 in
Height at shoulder: up to 6 ft 6 in

Bone stripper

The harsh life in the mountains provides a plentiful supply of dead animals for the huge Himalayan griffon vulture to eat. A group of these vultures can strip a small animal such as an antelope to the bone in only 20 minutes. Sometimes they eat so much at one meal that they are almost too heavy to take off again.

Trees on the mountainsides soak up rain and help to hold the soil together.

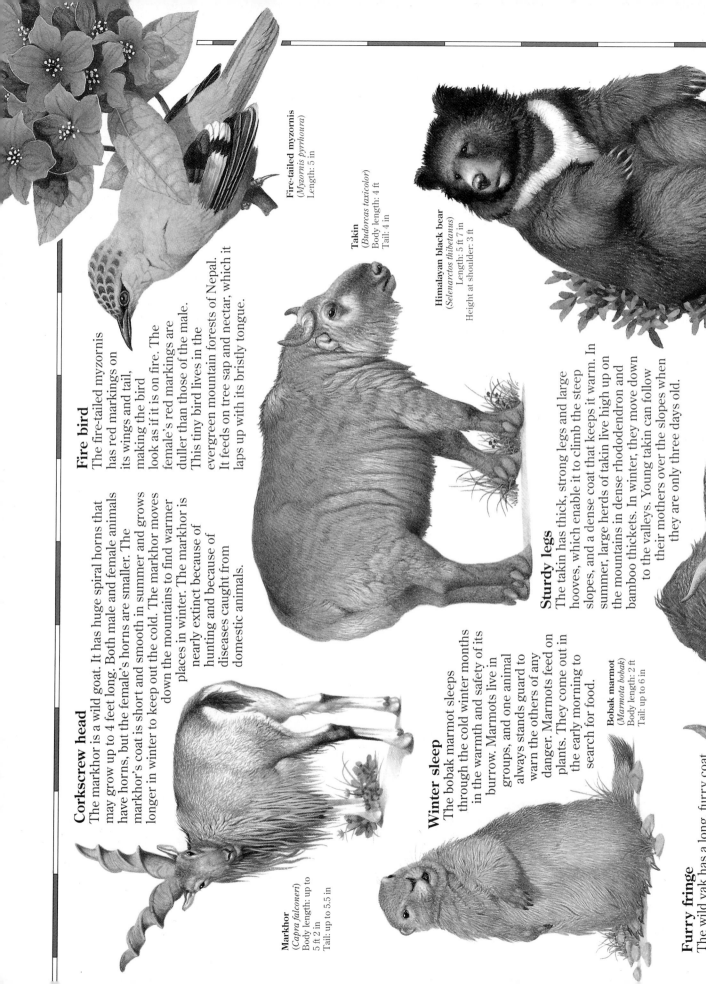

FIRE-TAILED MYZORNIS

BHUTAN GLORY

SNOW LEOPARD

BAY OF BENGAL

Ganges

S
A
Y
A

The Far East

CHINA IS ONE OF THE LARGEST COUNTRIES in the world. The climate over this vast area is controlled by the wet summer monsoon winds and the bitterly cold winds that blow down from the Arctic in winter. Two-thirds of the country is covered by mountains or desert, habitats which provide a refuge for some of the world's rarest animals, such as the giant panda and the Siberian tiger. China also has a rich birdlife, especially pheasants and cranes. In the east, much of the land is intensively cultivated to provide food for China's population of more than one billion people.

The islands of Japan stretch for over 1,200 miles off the east coast of China. Japan has a mild climate, with warm summers, cool winters, and plentiful rainfall. Broadleaved forests cover much of the land, despite dense areas of population.

Sika (*Cervus nippon*)
Length: up to 4 ft
Height at shoulder: up to 2 ft 8 in

Bamboo eater
The giant panda feeds mainly on bamboo. It munches its way through about 600 bamboo stems a day and spends up to 16 hours a day just eating. Below its first finger is a thumblike knob that helps to grasp the stems, and its throat has a tough lining that protects it from sharp splinters of bamboo. Each giant panda lives in its own territory in the misty mountain forests of southwest China. Its thick, waterproof fur keeps it warm and dry. Baby pandas are pink, blind, and helpless when they are born. They take their first steps when they are about three months old, but they cannot walk well until they are a year old.

White warning
The sika deer has a patch of white fur on its rump which it fluffs up when it is alarmed. This acts as a warning signal to other sika. In summer, the sika has a chestnut coat with white spots, which camouflages it among the trees. In winter, it grows darker fur and loses most of its spots. Sika are very hardy animals and have been introduced into parks and forests all over the world.

Courting collar
The male golden pheasant has a colorful collar of feathers which he displays during courtship to attract the female. He spreads the golden feathers forward like a fan until they cover his beak. Golden pheasants live in the forests of central China. They nest on the ground. After mating, the female rears the brood alone. She sits on the eggs to keep them warm and does not eat until they hatch some 22 days later. The newborn chicks can feed themselves as soon as they hatch and can fly when they are only a week old.

Golden pheasant
(*Chrysolophus pictus*)
Length including train:
up to 3 ft 3 in

Dinosaur-age ancestors
The tree shrew probably looks like the very first mammals that developed millions of years ago in the days of the dinosaurs. It is an active animal, always on the move and sniffing everything with its long, pointed nose. Tree shrews live in pairs, building a nest on the ground or among tree roots. The male marks his territory with a strong scent made by glands in his throat.

Common tree shrew
(*Tupaia glis*)
Body length:
up to 9 in
Tail: up to 9 in

Echo-sounder
The whitefin, or Chinese river dolphin, is one of the few dolphins that live in fresh water. It has poor eyesight and finds its food by sending out high-pitched sounds and waiting for the echo to bounce back. The time this takes helps the dolphin to work out the shape and distance of the object. The whitefin dolphin has about 130 sharp, pointed teeth, which it uses for spearing fish. It also probes in the mud with its long snout to look for shrimp.

Whitefin dolphin
(*Lipotes vexillifer*)
Length: up to 8 ft

Giant panda
(*Ailuropoda melanoleuca*)
Length: up to 5 ft

Hot baths
Japanese macaque monkeys live in troops of up to 40 individuals, led by an adult male. Troops that live in the cold, snowy mountains of northern Japan have learned to keep warm in winter by taking hot baths in the volcanic mountain springs. They sit right up to their necks in the water of the hot springs. Their dense fur also helps to keep them warm. Other troops of these intelligent monkeys have learned to wash sand off their food before eating it.

Japanese macaque (*Macaca fuscata*)
Length: up to 2 ft 6 in
Tail: up to 8 in

MILES
0   100   200   300   400

PACIFIC OCEAN

JAPANESE MACAQUE

SIKA

SEA OF JAPAN

J A P A N

JAPANESE GIANT SALAMANDER

Japanese giant salamander
(*Andrias japonicus*)
Length: up to 5 ft

Giant from the past
The huge Japanese giant salamander is the world's largest amphibian. Salamanders like this lived on Earth about 300 million years ago, but most of today's amphibians are much smaller. The giant salamander lives in cold streams, using folds of skin along the sides of its body to take in oxygen from the water. It also comes to the surface to take air into its lungs.

About 70 percent of Japan's land area is covered by mountainous forests.

The Huang He, or Yellow River, flows right across China. It contains a lot of silt, which gives the water a yellowish color.

KOREAN PENINSULA

EAST CHINA SEA

T A I W A N

SIBERIAN TIGER

Siberian tiger
(*Panthera tigris*)
Body length: up to 8 ft
Tail: up to 3 ft

Largest cat
The Siberian tiger is the largest and rarest of all the big cats. It is larger and furrier and has paler colors than tigers that live in India and Indonesia. There are probably only a few hundred Siberian tigers left in the wild. Tigers live on their own, marking the edge of their territories with scent, droppings, and scrape marks. They also roar to tell other tigers to keep away. A tiger's roars can be heard up to 2 miles away. Tigers come out at night to hunt for wild pigs, deer, and other forest animals.

Rare reptile
The timid Chinese alligator is threatened with extinction because people collect it for commercial breeding and because its marshland habitat is being destroyed. Today there are probably only a few hundred of these alligators left, and they inhabit only the lower part of the Chang Jiang, or Yangtze, river in eastern China. The Chinese alligator hibernates, or sleeps, in caves or burrows during the cold, dry winter months. It comes out in spring to mate and raise a family. This alligator feeds on snails, clams, rats, and insects.

Chinese alligator
(*Alligator sinensis*)
Length: up to 6 ft 6 in

CHINESE ALLIGATOR

WHITEFIN DOLPHIN

Lake Poyang

Lake Dongting

COMMON TREE SHREW

Xi Jiang

Huang He (Yellow River)

C H I N A

SOUTH CHINA SEA

Chang Jiang (Yangtze)

GOLDEN PHEASANT

MUSK DEER

GIANT PANDA

RED PANDA

HAINAN

Perfumed stomach
The male musk deer has a special gland under its stomach that produces a smelly substance called musk in the breeding season. Many musk deer have been killed to obtain this gland, which is used to make the musky aroma of perfumes. The male has canine teeth about 3 inches long which stick out of the sides of his mouth. In the breeding season, rival males fight by showing these teeth and wrestling with their necks to fend off bites.

Musk deer
(*Moschus moschiferus*)
Body length: 3 ft 3 in
Height at shoulder: 2 ft 2 in

The bamboo forests of Sichuan province in southwest China are home to the rare giant panda.

Red panda (*Ailurus fulgens*)
Body length: up to 2 ft 1 in
Tail: up to 19 in

Climbing panda
The red panda comes out at night, using its sharp claws to climb quickly through the trees. It feeds mainly on bamboo shoots, roots, grasses, and fruit. It often washes itself like a cat, licking a foot and then wiping the wet foot over its fur. Young red pandas can look after themselves when they are a few months old, but they stay with their mother for over a year.

Southeastern Asia and India

THE CLIMATE IN INDIA is dominated by the seasonal changes caused by the monsoon winds. They bring torrential rain and violent storms in summer. Dry, cooler weather occurs in winter. Indian animals, such as the elephant and rhinoceros, are similar to animals found in southeastern Asia or Africa.

The climate of southeastern Asia is generally warm and humid all year round, and tropical rainforests flourish. Many animals live high up in the canopy of the forest where there is more light, water, and food. Several animals, such as the colugo, glide between the trees on "wings" of skin. These rainforests are also home to one of our closest living relatives – the orangutan – and to a huge number of insects, many of which reach a spectacular size. Much of the original rainforest has been cleared to make way for farmland and houses, so many animals are in danger of extinction. Some of the rarest animals, such as the Javan rhinoceros, survive only in remote parts of the Indonesian islands.

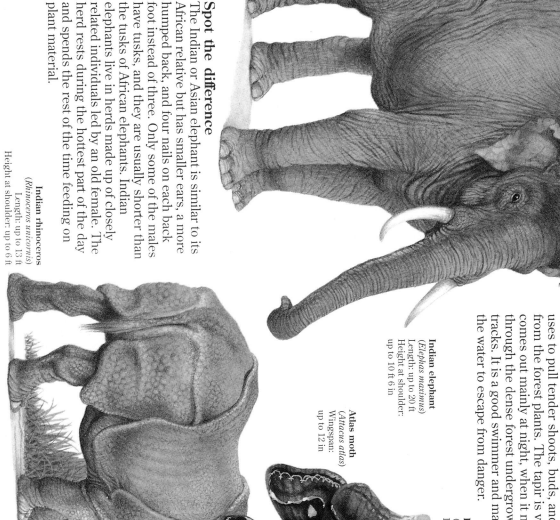

Spot the difference
The Indian or Asian elephant is similar to its African relative but has smaller ears, a more humped back, and four nails on each back foot instead of three. Only some of the males have tusks, and they are usually shorter than the tusks of African elephants. Indian elephants live in herds made up of closely related individuals led by an old female. The herd rests during the hottest part of the day and spends the rest of the time feeding on plant material.

Indian elephant
(*Elephas maximus*)
Length: up to 20 ft
Height at shoulder:
up to 10 ft 6 in

Indian rhinoceros
(*Rhinoceros unicornis*)
Length: up to 13 ft
Height at shoulder: up to 6 ft

Handy nose
The Malayan tapir has a long snout that it uses to pull tender shoots, buds, and fruits from the forest plants. The tapir is very timid and comes out mainly at night, when it moves quickly through the dense forest undergrowth on well-worn tracks. It is a good swimmer and may plunge into the water to escape from danger.

Malayan tapir
(*Tapirus indicus*)
Length: 6 ft 6 in
Height at shoulder 3 ft 3 in

Armor plating
The Indian rhinoceros looks as if it is wearing a suit of armor because it has thick, knobby skin with deep folds at the joints. This skin protects the rhino from spiky forest plants. The rhinoceros usually lives on its own and likes to be near water, as it often takes baths. The Indian rhinoceros has been hunted almost to extinction for its horn, which is used in Chinese folk medicine.

Wings with eyes
The eyespots on the wingtips of the huge atlas moth look like eyes on the head of a snake. This mimicry protects the moth from attack by birds and other predators. Many moths have eyespots that frighten birds away or divert their attack to the edges of the wings. The male atlas moth has large, feathery antennae which pick up the scent given off by females that are ready to mate. This helps him to find a female among the forest trees.

Atlas moth
(*Attacus atlas*)
Wingspan:
up to 12 in

Hooded poisoner
The king cobra has huge poison glands. A bite from this snake can kill an elephant in four hours, and a person in just 15 to 20 minutes. King cobras are usually secretive and quiet animals, but they can be aggressive when defending their eggs. To frighten off an intruder, the king cobra hisses, raises the front of its body, and spreads out the skin around its neck to form a hood.

King cobra
(*Ophiophagus hannah*)
Length: up to 18 ft

MILES
0   150   300   450   600

BLUE
PEACOCK

INDIAN
ELEPHANT

KING
COBRA

INDIAN
RHINOCEROS

I N D I A

Indus

Narmada

Krishna

Godavari

Ganges

SRI
LANKA

A R A B I A N   S E A

B A Y   O F   B E N G A L

Feather fan

The male blue peacock spreads out his long tail feathers in an enormous, quivering fan to attract a peahen. The huge staring "eyes" on his feathers may serve to hypnotize the peahen and allow the male to mate with her. In the breeding season, the male defends his territory against other males. Fights can last a whole day or more, but the birds do not often injure each other. After the breeding season is over, the male's tail feathers fall out.

Blue peacock
(*Pavo cristatus*)
Body length: 2 ft 6 in
Tail: 5 ft

Giant dragon

The rare Komodo dragon is the largest lizard in the world. It feeds on small deer, monkeys, goats, and wild boar, and it has even attacked and killed people. The dragon has a flexible skull that enables it to swallow large pieces of food whole. It flicks its bright yellow tongue in and out to taste its food and to sense odors.

Komodo dragon
(*Varanus komodoensis*)
Length: up to 10 ft

Smallest mammal

The tiny Kitti's hog-nosed bat is the smallest mammal in the world. It is sometimes called the "bumblebee bat" because it is no bigger than a bee. Kitti's hog-nosed bat is very rare and lives only in a few isolated caves in the rainforests of Thailand. It was first discovered by scientists in 1973. This bat has a pig-like nose which may help it to snatch insects and other invertebrates from the surface of leaves.

Kitti's hog-nosed bat
(*Craseonycteris thonglongyai*)
Length: 1.3 in
Wingspan: 4.7 in

Mudskipper
(*Periophthalmus chrysospilus*)
Length: 9 in

Orangutan
(*Pongo pygmaeus*)
Height: up to 5 ft

Swinging arms

The orangutan has long, muscular arms that reach down to its ankles. Its arms swing rapidly hand-over-hand as it moves through the trees. On the ground, the orangutan stands upright or walks on all fours. At night, it sleeps in a tree in a nest made of sticks. The name orang-utan means "jungle man" in the Malay language.

Colugo
(*Cynocephalus volans*)
Body length: up to 16.5 in
Tail: up to 10.5 in

Skin wings

The colugo, or flying lemur, glides from one rainforest tree to another using thin "wings" of skin that stretch between its arms, legs, and tail. The colugo climbs awkwardly up tree trunks because its folded wings get in the way. On the ground it is helpless and cannot even stand up. A young colugo clings to its mother's belly as she glides through the forest.

Aerial view of rainforest on the island of Borneo.

The woodlands of northern India are home to many animals and birds.

Mangrove swamps grow along the coasts of India and many of the islands of southeastern Asia.

COLUGO

SULAWESI

BORNEO

PROBOSCIS MONKEY

MUDSKIPPER

ORANGUTAN

KOMODO DRAGON

S O U T H E A S T E R N   A S I A

Mekong

Salween

KITTI'S HOG-NOSED BAT

ATLAS MOTH

MALAYAN TAPIR

SUMATRA

Irrawaddy

BAY OF BENGAL

Walking fish

The mudskipper uses its fleshy fins like arms to pull itself over the mud of the mangrove swamps. It can also "skip" over the mud by suddenly bending the back part of its body. When the tide rises, the mudskipper climbs up a tree and clings to the branches using a "sucker" made from two of its rear fins joined together.

Proboscis monkey
(*Nasalis larvatus*)
Length: up to 2 ft 6 in
Tail: up to 2 ft 6 in

Loudspeaker nose

The male proboscis monkey has a very large nose which gets in the way when he eats. This nose probably acts as a loudspeaker for the male's honking calls, which warn other proboscis monkeys of danger. The nose straightens out during each honk and swells or goes red if the monkey gets angry or excited. The proboscis monkey is very agile, leaping through the mangrove forests using its long tail as a counterbalance. Its long fingers and toes help it to grip the branches.

The Outback

THE DRY, DESERTLIKE PLAINS of the Australian outback cover more than two-thirds of the continent. Much of the region receives less than 10 inches of rainfall a year, and the rains may come at any time of the year. There are often long periods of drought, which make it difficult for animals to survive.

Many animals avoid the heat of the day by staying in their burrows, as it is cooler and moister underground. Some small animals sleep underground right through the hottest summer months. This is known as estivation. Many outback animals can survive with little or no water. Their bodies are adapted to store water from their food and to lose very little water in their urine. A number of animals have long back legs which allow them to move rapidly and find what food is available.

Frightening frill

When a frilled lizard is attacked, it suddenly spreads the flap of skin around its neck. This makes it look four times as big and much more dangerous than it really is. The bright color inside its mouth also scares attackers away.

Frilled lizard
(*Chlamydosaurus kingii*)
Length including tail: 3 ft 3 in

Spiny coat

The echidna's long, sharp spines help to protect it from predators. If it is attacked, it rolls itself into a ball or digs straight down into the soil. In this way it hides its soft face and underparts, where there are no spines.

Rabbit-eared bandicoot
(*Macrotis lagotis*)
Length including tail: 18 in

Incubator bird

The male mallee fowl builds a huge compost heap in which the female lays her eggs. The heat given off by the rotting compost keeps the eggs warm. The male bird tests the temperature with his tongue and the skin inside his mouth. When the chicks hatch, they have to push their way up to the surface.

Mallee fowl
(*Leipoa ocellata*)
Length: 2 ft

Echidna
(*Tachyglossus aculeatus*)
Length: 20 in
Spines: 2 in

Deep digger

The rabbit-eared bandicoot uses its strong claws to dig burrows up to 6 feet deep. The female's pouch opens from the tail side; this keeps dirt off her baby. To escape the heat of day, bandicoots stay in their burrows.

High-speed runner

Emus cannot fly, but they have strong legs and massive feet and can run up to 30 mph. The emu is the second largest bird in the world (the ostrich is the largest). Emus usually eat grass, berries, fruit, and insects but they have been known to swallow marbles, nails, and coins. The male emu incubates the eggs for about eight weeks, and during this time he loses nearly 18 pounds in weight. When the chicks hatch, they follow their father around for about 18 months.

Emu
(*Dromaius novaehollandiae*)
Height: 6 ft 6 in

Giant hunter

The perentie is one of the largest lizards in the world. It has powerful jaws, sharp, curved teeth, and huge claws. It is able to catch snakes, other lizards, rabbits, birds, and even small kangaroos. To defend itself, the perentie lashes its heavy tail from side to side.

Perentie
(*Varanus giganteus*)
Length including tail: up to 8 ft

Bottle trees survive in dry areas by storing water under their bark.

Ayers Rock, in central Australia, is the world's largest freestanding rock.

INDIAN OCEAN

GREAT SANDY DESERT

GIBSON DESERT

GREAT VICTORIA DESERT

NULLARBOR PLAIN

GREAT AUSTRALIAN BIGHT

AUSTRALIA

Lake Amadeus

Lake Eyre

Lake Torrens

Lake Gairdner

EMU

WOMBAT

DINGO

MALLEE FOWL

RABBIT-EARED BANDICOOT

WATER-HOLDING FROG

MARSUPIAL MOLE

ECHIDNA

FRILLED LIZARD

Tunnel dweller

The marsupial mole uses its long claws to dig tunnels in soft sand dunes. Its body is a smooth, streamlined shape and it pushes easily through the sand. Its nose is protected by a horny shield. The mole spends all its life underground in dark tunnels, so it has no eyes.

Marsupial mole
(*Notoryctes typhlops*)
Length: up to 6 in

Mulgara
(*Dasycercus cristicauda*)
Length including tail:
up to 12 in

Long jumper

Red kangaroos bound along on their enormous back legs and use their strong tails to help them balance. Some of the big males can clear more than 30 feet in one leap. Only the males have red fur. The females are blue-gray in color. Red kangaroos are able to survive the high temperatures and scarcity of water in the outback.

Red kangaroo
(*Macropus rufus*)
Height: 6 ft 6 in
Tail: 3 ft 3 in

Fast food

Mulgaras eat up to 25 percent of their own weight in meat every day. They rush at mice, birds, and small lizards and kill them almost instantly. Mulgaras hardly ever drink and avoid the heat of the day by staying in their burrows.

Scary tongue

When the blue-tongued skinks is frightened, it sticks out its bright blue tongue and makes a hissing sound. Although this display may help to scare off attackers, the skink is really quite harmless.

Blue-tongued skink
(*Tiliqua scincoides*)
Length: 20 in

Desert devil

The thorny devil, or moloch, is a type of lizard. It is covered with hard spines which protect it from attack. It gets liquid from dew which forms on its skin at night. The dew runs along thousands of tiny grooves on the lizard's skin and collects in its mouth.

Thorny devil
(*Moloch horridus*)
Length including
tail: 6 in

Wild dog

Dingos are descended from domesticated dogs that people brought to Australia about 8,000 years ago, but they have become wild again. Dingos have larger canine teeth than domesticated dogs.

Dingo (*Canis dingo*)
Height to shoulder: 20 in
Length: up to 3 ft

Water tank

The water-holding frog stores water in its bladder. A large frog can hold half its own weight in water. It also produces a special outer layer of skin that forms a watery cocoon around its body. This helps it to survive through drought until the rains come again.

Water-holding frog
(*Cyclorana platycephalus*)
Length: 2 in

Huge burrows

The wombat avoids the heat of the day by staying in a deep burrow, which can be up to 100 feet long. The entrance may be 6 feet wide. Wombats feed on grass and can go without water for months at a time.

Wombat
(*Vombatus ursinus*)
Height at shoulder: 18 in

CORAL SEA

PACIFIC OCEAN

GREAT DIVIDING RANGE

BASS STRAIT

TASMANIA

Darling

Murray

I A

MILES
0   200   400

THORNY DEVIL

PERENTIE

MULGARA

BLUE-TONGUED SKINK

RED KANGAROO

Termite nests are common in the outback and may be up to 20 feet high.

Rainforests and Woods

THE LUXURIANT TROPICAL RAINFORESTS of northeastern Australia are a striking contrast to the dry interior of the continent. They are hot and damp, providing a home for an unusual variety of animals, from tree kangaroos to spectacular birds of paradise. Similar wildlife thrives in the misty mountain forests of New Guinea, a Pacific island about 1,500 miles long that lies northeast of Australia.

In the southwest and southeast of Australia there are cooler, drier eucalyptus woods, where rain falls mainly during the winter and early spring. Many birds nest there in the winter months. The eucalyptus trees and other flowering trees and shrubs are a rich source of fruit, nuts, and nectar for birds and many other creatures. The animals, in turn, carry pollen from plant to plant, fertilizing the flowers.

Funnel-web spider
(*Atrax robustus*)
Length: 1 in

Silky killer
The funnel-web spider lives in a burrow with an entrance shaped like a funnel. It lines the burrow with a silky web. At night, the spider emerges to seize insects that are ensnared in its web. It injects poison into its victims through its fangs. The funnel-web is one of the few spiders that can kill people with its venom.

Furry parachute
The sugar glider has extra skin between its front and back legs. It spreads its limbs to glide from tree to tree like a living parachute, steering with its tail. It can cover 165 feet in one glide. The sugar glider feeds on insects, nectar, fruit, and the sweet, sugary sap of the eucalyptus tree, from which this glider gets its name.

Rainbow lorikeet
(*Trichoglossus haematodus*)
Length: 12 in

Dancing display
The rainbow lorikeet performs a dance of special hopping and preening movements to warn other lorikeets to keep out of its territory. The male uses a similar display to win a female during courtship.

Sugar glider
(*Petaurus breviceps*)
Body length: 8 in
Tail: 8 in

Taipan
(*Oxyuranus scutellatus*)
Length: up to 12 ft

Nonslip soles
The tree kangaroo has wide paws with rough pads and sharp, curved claws, which help it grip as it climbs. Its long tail enables it to balance on branches and also acts as a rudder when the kangaroo leaps from branch to branch.

Tree kangaroo
(*Dendrolagus lumholtzi*)
Body length: up to
2 ft 6 in
Tail: up to 3 ft

Powerful poison
The taipan is one of the most poisonous snakes in the world. One taipan has enough venom (poison) to kill 125,000 mice. A bite of its sharp fangs can kill an adult human being within minutes. Although the taipan is shy, it becomes fierce when it is threatened.

Western spinebill
(*Acanthorhynchus superciliosus*)
Length: 6 in
Bill: 1 in

Nectar eater
The western spinebill uses its long, curved bill to probe for nectar in flowers. It gathers the nectar with a brush at the tip of its tongue. To suck the nectar, the spinebill rolls up the sides of its tongue and uses it as a straw.

Many palm trees grow on Australia's coastal plain.

Rainforest on the mountains of the Great Dividing Range.

Dense rainforest vegetation in eastern New Guinea.

QUEEN ALEXANDRA'S BIRDWING BUTTERFLY

INDIAN OCEAN

WESTERN SPINEBILL

NUMBAT

HONEY POSSUM

Gascoyne

Ashburton

AUSTRALIA

TANAMI DESERT

SIMPSON DESERT

Lake Amadeus

▲ Ayers Rock

Lake Eyre

Lake Torrens

Lake Gairdner

GREAT AUSTRALIAN BIGHT

FLINDERS RANGES

RAINBOW LORIKEET

N E W

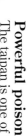

MILES
0
200
400

Queen Alexandra's birdwing butterfly
(*Ornithoptera alexandrae*)
Wingspan: up to 11 in

Biggest butterfly
The Queen Alexandra's birdwing butterfly is the world's largest butterfly. It is now very rare because of overcollecting and the destruction of the rainforests. This butterfly usually flies high above the ground, among the sunlit, flowering treetops.

Invisible lizard
During the daytime, the leaf-tailed gecko is perfectly camouflaged against the mossy tree trunks in the rainforests. With its flattened shape, it casts few shadows, and the outline of its body is blurred by the frills along its sides.

Leaf-tailed gecko
(*Phyllurus cornutus*)
Length: 12 in

Fantastic feathers
The male Raggiana bird of paradise shows off his spectacular feathers to compete against other males and win a female. His performance may include hanging upside down from a branch. The female bird of paradise is very plain-looking.

Kookaburra
(*Dacelo gigas*)
Length: 17 in

Alarm clock bird
The kookaburra's noisy, laughing call tells other kookaburras to keep out of its territory. Kookaburras often call at dawn and wake people up. They feed mainly on mice, insects, and small snakes.

Leafy diet
The koala has a very specialized diet – it eats only the leaves of certain types of eucalyptus trees. It has cheek pouches for storing the leaves and an extralong intestine for digesting them. The koala gets most of its moisture from its food and rarely drinks water. Its name comes from an Aboriginal (native Australian) word meaning "no drink." The koala is good at climbing trees. Its knifelike claws can grip the bark, and its fingers and toes can curl around the branches.

Koala
(*Phascolarctos cinereus*)
Length: 2 ft 8 in

Raggiana bird of paradise
(*Paradisaea raggiana*)
Body length: up to 3 ft 1 in
Tail feathers: 20 in

Honey possum
(*Tarsipes spenserae*)
Body length: 3 in

Flower feeder
The honey possum uses its long snout to probe into flowers for pollen, nectar, and insects. It has a long, thin tongue tipped with bristles for soaking up its food.

Toothy mammal
The numbat has a long tongue which it uses to lick up termites and ants. It has about 50 teeth – more than any other land mammal.

Numbat
(*Myrmecobius fasciatus*)
Body length: up to 12 in
Tail: up to 8 in

PACIFIC OCEAN

GUINEA

RAGGIANA BIRD OF PARADISE

SUGAR GLIDER

TREE KANGAROO

TAIPAN

LEAF-TAILED GECKO

KOALA

GREAT DIVIDING RANGE

KOOKABURRA

FUNNEL-WEB SPIDER

Murray

Darling

The Barrier Reef

THE BIGGEST coral reef in the world is the Great Barrier Reef, which stretches for nearly 1,250 miles along the northeastern coast of Australia. Tiny animals called corals have formed the reef. Over millions of years, the limestone skeletons of dead corals have built up on top of previous skeletons to make a reef. Coral reefs form only in warm, salty waters that are shallow enough for sunlight to reach the living corals.

Many living animals find food and shelter among the corals. The Great Barrier Reef is home to a large variety of creatures, including more than 1,500 species of fish, 350 species of coral, and many types of sponge.

AUSTRALIA

CAPE YORK PENINSULA

GREAT BARRIER REEF

GREAT BARRIER REEF MARINE PARK

LEAFY SEA DRAGON

GIANT CLAM

CLEANER FISH

CROWN-OF-THORNS STARFISH

CLOWNFISH AND SEA ANEMONE

BUTTERFLY FISH

GOLDEN TUBASTREA

GREAT BARRIER REEF MARINE PARK

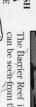
When coral is not covered by seawater it loses its bright colors.

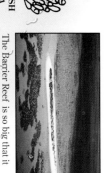
Underwater view of sea lilies, corals, and sponges.

The Barrier Reef is so big that it can be seen from the moon.

M I L E S
0   50   100

Hinged shell

The giant clam weighs up to 500 pounds. Its shell is in two parts, joined by a hinge. The clam keeps its shell open to filter food from the water. But if danger threatens, its powerful muscle quickly snaps the shell shut. A giant clam can trap the arm or leg of an unwary diver.

Giant clam
(*Tridacna gigas*)
Width of shell:
up to 5 ft

Attractive patterns

The bright colors and patterns of the butterfly fish help it to recognize others of its own species and to attract a mate. The many kinds of butterfly fish do not compete. Each species prefers a different environment and its own variety of food.

Butterfly fish (*Chaetodon auriga*)
Length: up to 8 in

Free food

The cleaner fish gets a free meal from other fishes on the reef. It nibbles parasites and dead scales from their skin, and food particles from their teeth. Its odd dance draws a crowd of fish for a cleaning. None try to eat it.

Cleaner fish (*Labroides dimidiatus*)
Length: up to 12 in

Special friends

Sea anemones have poisonous tentacles that kill small fishes for food. The clownfish is not harmed by this poison and lives among the tentacles, where it is safe from predators. In turn, the clownfish lures other fish to the anemone's tentacles.

Reef wrecker

The crown-of-thorns starfish eats coral by turning its stomach inside out through the mouth and pressing the stomach lining against the coral surfaces. The soft coral parts are digested, and the skeletons are left behind. These starfish do great damage to the reef. Each one can kill 20 square feet of coral a day.

Crown-of-thorns starfish (*Acanthaster planci*)
Diameter: up to 2 ft

Stinging tentacles

The golden tubastrea coral looks like a plant, but it is really an animal. It uses stinging cells on its tentacles to catch tiny living things floating in the water.

Golden tubastrea
(*Tubastrea aurea*)
Diameter of each
coral: 0.35 in

Seaweed dragon

The leafy sea dragon is a type of seahorse. It is covered with ragged flaps of skin that make it look like a piece of floating seaweed rather than a tasty fish. Like other seahorses, the male sea dragon carries the eggs in a special pouch on his body until they hatch.

Leafy sea dragon
(*Phyllopteryx eques*)
Length: up to 10 in

Sea anemone (*Stoichactis*)
Diameter: up to 3 ft 3 in

Clownfish
(*Amphiprion percula*)
Length: 3 in

Tasmania

THE ISLAND OF TASMANIA was once part of mainland Australia, but it is now separated from southeastern Australia by the Bass Strait. Tasmania has a cool, wet climate. The western part of the island contains large areas of rainforest that are home to many animals. Tasmania's isolation has allowed some animals to develop into unusual forms or separate species. Many rare animals live in the area around the Gordon and Franklin rivers in the southwest, which is unusual in having no cats, rats, or dogs.

These mammals were brought to Australia and Tasmania by people, and have wiped out many of the native pouched mammals and birds in other areas.

Reluctant flier
The ground parrot spends most of its time on the ground. It can fly, but rarely goes more than 650 feet before landing. The parrot is active at night, when there is less danger from predators.

Ground parrot
(*Pezoporus wallicus*)
Length: 12 in

Big mouth
The tiger cat is a pouched mammal that hunts mostly at night. Its jaws can open very wide and it has big, pointed teeth. The tiger cat's sharp claws and ridged pads on the back paws make it a superb tree climber.

Tiger cat
(*Dasyurops maculatus*)
Height at shoulder: 12 in
Body length: 2 ft 3 in

Forest demon
The Tasmanian devil's name comes from its black color and eerie, whining snarl. The animal has strong jaws and teeth that can crush bones. It eats its entire prey – fur or feathers, skin and bones – until nothing is left. Tasmanian devils are very shy and usually run away from people.

Tasmanian devil
(*Sarcophilus harrisi*)
Height at shoulder: 12 in
Body length: 2 ft 3 in

Rare wolf
The thylacine, or Tasmanian wolf, is thought to be extinct, but a few may still survive in remote parts of Tasmania. The thylacine is a pouched mammal with doglike feet and teeth. It whines, barks, and growls like a dog, but it has a thick tail like a kangaroo's. It can kill animals as large as a sheep.

Thylacine
(*Thylacinus cynocephalus*)
Body length: 4 ft
Tail: 2 ft

Bony bill
The platypus is a very unusual mammal because it lays eggs. Its bill is really a flat snout made of bone and rubbery skin. When swimming under water, the platypus shuts its ears and eyes and uses its bill to probe in the mud for food. It can stay under water for up to five minutes.

Platypus
(*Ornithorhynchus anatinus*)
Length including tail: 21 in
Bill: 4 in

Tunneling wallaby
The red-bellied pademelon is a type of kangaroo that makes tunnels through the tangled undergrowth. It lives in large groups and builds complicated networks of tunnels, like rabbit warrens. If a pademelon is alarmed, it may thump the ground with its hind legs to warn other pademelons of approaching danger.

Red-bellied pademelon
(*Thylogale billardieri*)
Height: 2 ft 3 in
Tail: 16 in

BASS STRAIT

KING ISLAND

INDIAN OCEAN

TASMAN SEA

TASMANIA

Many of the mountainous areas of Tasmania are covered by forest.

Thick vegetation covers the banks of the Franklin River in southwestern Tasmania.

Great Lake

Lake Mackintosh

Lake Gordon

PLATYPUS

RED-BELLIED PADEMELON

THYLACINE

TASMANIAN DEVIL

TIGER CAT

GROUND PARROT

MILES
0 10 20 30

New Zealand

THE ISLANDS of New Zealand lie about 1,000 miles east of Australia. North Island is dominated by a central volcanic plateau, while South Island is mostly mountainous, with glaciers and fjords (bays bordered by steep cliffs). Forests and grasslands flourish in the cool, wet climate.

New Zealand split off from the other landmasses before mammals became a major group of animals. There are only two mammals native to the country, both of them bats. New Zealand's birds are able to live in habitats that elsewhere are used by mammals. Many flightless birds have survived there because they have had so few mammal enemies.

Crawling bat
The rare New Zealand short-tailed bat is good at moving around on the ground and can run fast on all fours, even up steep slopes. It has large, wide feet with wrinkled soles for a firmer grip.

Leiopelma hamiltoni
Length: up to 2 in

Kea
(*Nestor notabilis*)
Length: 18 in

Ancient frog
Ancestors of the rare frog *Leiopelma hamiltoni* lived 150 million years ago. This frog has no eardrums or vocal sac. It does not have a tadpole stage, but becomes a tailed froglet within the egg. The froglet thrashes its tail to break out.

Short-tailed bat
(*Mystacina tuberculata*)
Length: up to 2 in

Furry feathers
The brown kiwi is a flightless bird covered in long feathers that look like shaggy fur. It lives in a burrow and comes out at night to hunt for worms and insects. The kiwi finds its prey with its acute hearing and the nostrils on the tip of its sensitive bill.

Brown kiwi
(*Apteryx australis*)
Height: 14 in
Bill: 6 in

Snow parrot
The kea is an unusual parrot that lives in the snowy Southern Alps. It uses its beak to dig up roots and shoots under the snow, but it also eats meat. It has been known to tear hikers' boots and to eat campers' tents to shreds.

Tuatara
(*Sphenodon punctatus*)
Length: up to 2 ft

In the Southern Alps are many lakes, which were carved out by glaciers during the Ice Age.

KAKAPO

STEWART ISLAND

SHORT-TAILED BAY

KEA

SOUTH ISLAND

SOUTHERN ALPS

CANTERBURY PLAINS

Evergreen trees and tree ferns are the most common plants in New Zealand's forests.

Kakapo
(*Strigops habroptilus*)
Length: 2 ft 1 in

TASMAN SEA

TASMAN MTS

TASMAN BAY

LEIOPELMA HAMILTONI

COOK STRAIT

PACIFIC OCEAN

Special survivor
The tuatara is related to reptiles that lived during the age of the dinosaurs. The male can raise the spines on his back to scare off predators. The name tuatara means "peaks on the back" in the Maori language (spoken in New Zealand). Tuataras can live for 120 years.

Flightless parrot
The kakapo, or owl parrot, is the only parrot in the world that cannot fly. It uses its short wings only to glide down from trees, but it can run fast. It comes out at night to search for berries, roots, leaves, and lizards.

TARARUA RANGE

BROWN KIWI

NORTH ISLAND

TUATARA

Lake Taupo

BAY OF PLENTY

RAUKUMARA RANGE

HAWKE BAY

Land on the slopes of the eastern hills of North Island is used for grazing sheep and dairy cattle.

MILES
0   25   50   75   100

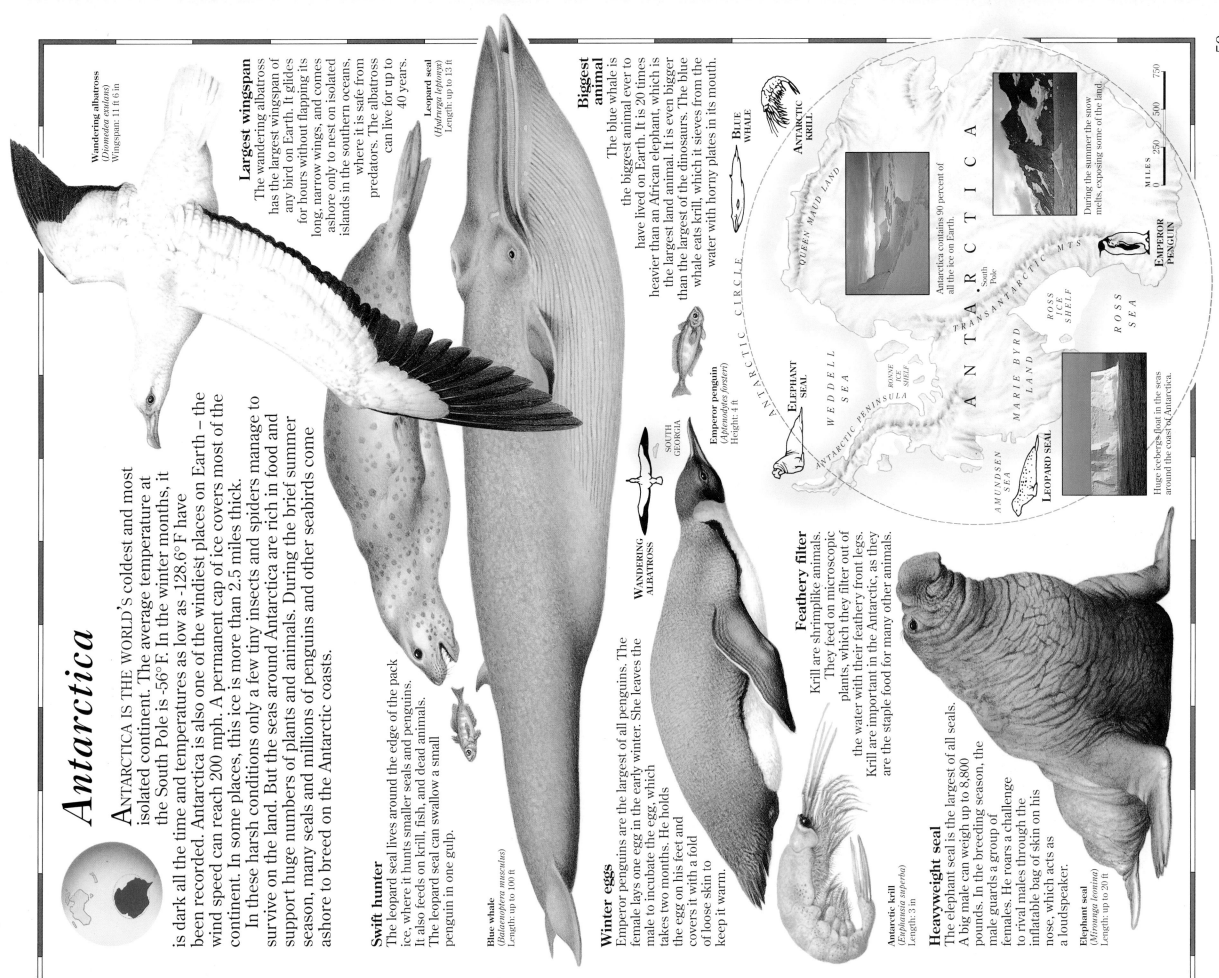

Antarctica

ANTARCTICA IS THE WORLD'S coldest and most isolated continent. The average temperature at the South Pole is -56°F. In the winter months, it is dark all the time and temperatures as low as -128.6°F have been recorded. Antarctica is also one of the windiest places on Earth – the wind speed can reach 200 mph. A permanent cap of ice covers most of the continent. In some places, this ice is more than 2.5 miles thick.

In these harsh conditions only a few tiny insects and spiders manage to survive on the land. But the seas around Antarctica are rich in food and support huge numbers of plants and animals. During the brief summer season, many seals and millions of penguins and other seabirds come ashore to breed on the Antarctic coasts.

Swift hunter
The leopard seal lives around the edge of the pack ice, where it hunts smaller seals and penguins. It also feeds on krill, fish, and dead animals. The leopard seal can swallow a small penguin in one gulp.

Blue whale
(Balaenoptera musculus)
Length: up to 100 ft

Winter eggs
Emperor penguins are the largest of all penguins. The female lays one egg in the early winter. She leaves the egg, which takes two months. He holds the egg on his feet and covers it with a fold of loose skin to keep it warm.

Antarctic krill
(Euphausia superba)
Length: 3 in

Heavyweight seal
The elephant seal is the largest of all seals. A big male can weigh up to 8,800 pounds. In the breeding season, the male guards a group of females. He roars a challenge to rival males through the inflatable bag of skin on his nose, which acts as a loudspeaker.

Elephant seal
(Mirounga leonina)
Length: up to 20 ft

Feathery filter
Krill are shrimplike animals. They feed on microscopic plants, which they filter out of the water with their feathery front legs. Krill are important in the Antarctic, as they are the staple food for many other animals.

Emperor penguin
(Aptenodytes forsteri)
Height: 4 ft

Biggest animal
The blue whale is the biggest animal ever to have lived on Earth. It is 20 times heavier than an African elephant, which is the largest land animal. It is even bigger than the largest of the dinosaurs. The blue whale eats krill, which it sieves from the water with horny plates in its mouth.

Wandering albatross
(Diomedea exulans)
Wingspan: 11 ft 6 in

Largest wingspan
The wandering albatross has the largest wingspan of any bird on Earth. It glides for hours without flapping its long, narrow wings, and comes ashore only to nest on isolated islands in the southern oceans, where it is safe from predators. The albatross can live for up to 40 years.

Leopard seal
(Hydrurga leptonyx)
Length: up to 13 ft

BLUE WHALE

ANTARCTIC KRILL

EMPEROR PENGUIN

ELEPHANT SEAL

LEOPARD SEAL

WANDERING ALBATROSS

SOUTH GEORGIA

QUEEN MAUD LAND

ANTARCTIC CIRCLE

TRANSANTARCTIC MTS

South Pole

A N T A R C T I C A

RONNE ICE SHELF

ROSS ICE SHELF

ROSS SEA

WEDDELL SEA

MARIE BYRD LAND

AMUNDSEN SEA

ANTARCTIC PENINSULA

Antarctica contains 90 percent of all the ice on Earth.

During the summer the snow melts, exposing some of the land.

Huge icebergs float in the seas around the coast of Antarctica.

MILES 0   250   500   750

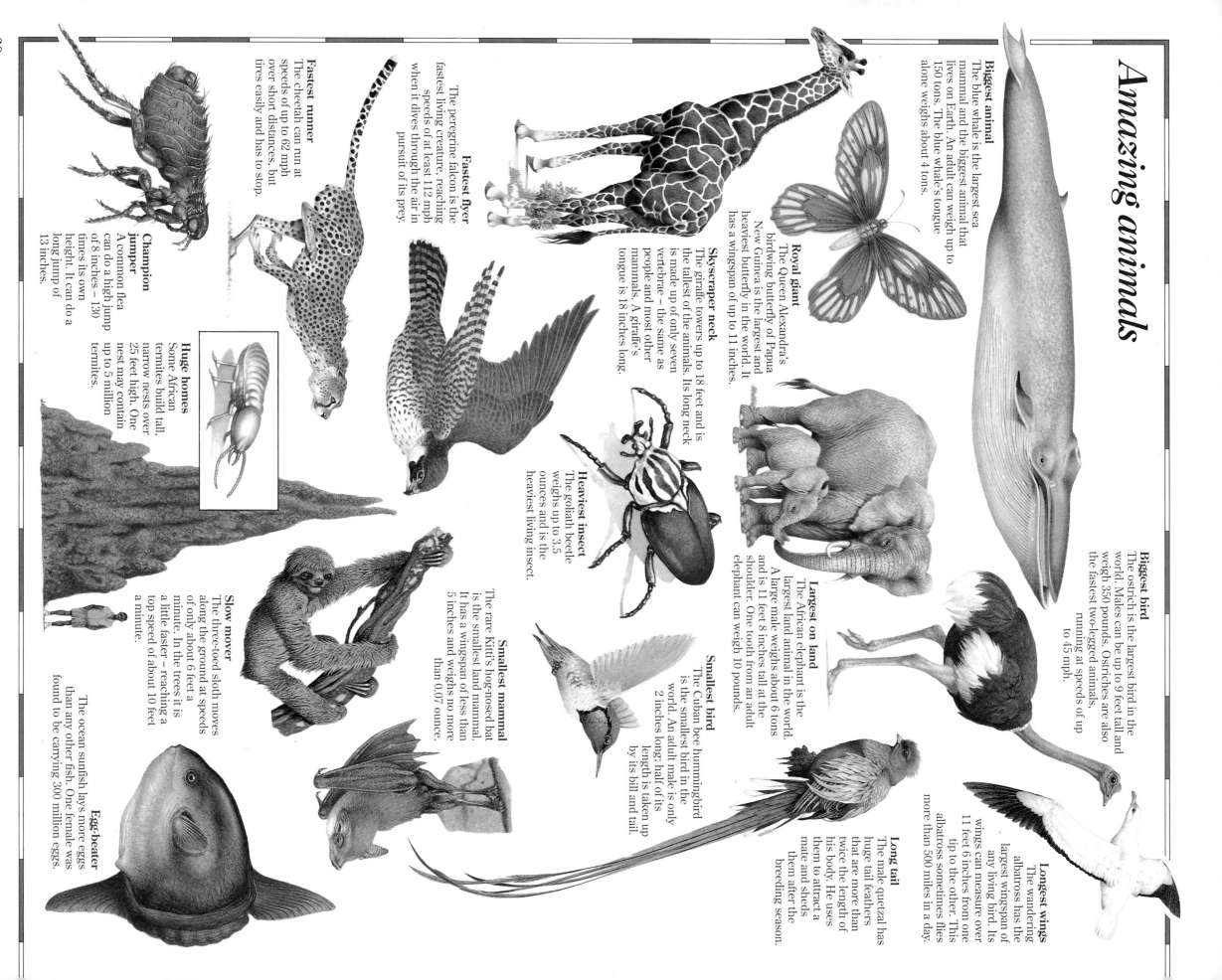

Amazing animals

Biggest animal
The blue whale is the largest sea mammal and the biggest animal that lives on Earth. An adult can weigh up to 150 tons. The blue whale's tongue alone weighs about 4 tons.

Fastest runner
The cheetah can run at speeds of up to 62 mph over short distances, but tires easily and has to stop.

Fastest flyer
The peregrine falcon is the fastest living creature, reaching speeds of at least 112 mph when it dives through the air in pursuit of its prey.

Champion jumper
A common flea can do a high jump of 8 inches – 130 times its own height. It can do a long jump of 13 inches.

Huge homes
Some African termites build tall, narrow nests over 25 feet high. One nest may contain up to 5 million termites.

Royal giant
The Queen Alexandra's birdwing butterfly of Papua New Guinea is the largest and heaviest butterfly in the world. It has a wingspan of up to 11 inches.

Skyscraper neck
The giraffe towers up to 18 feet and is the tallest of the animals. Its long neck is made up of only seven vertebrae – the same as people and most other mammals. A giraffe's tongue is 18 inches long.

Heaviest insect
The goliath beetle weighs up to 3.5 ounces and is the heaviest living insect.

Largest on land
The African elephant is the largest land animal in the world. A large male weighs about 6 tons and is 11 feet 8 inches tall at the shoulder. One tooth from an adult elephant can weigh 10 pounds.

Smallest bird
The Cuban bee hummingbird is the smallest bird in the world. An adult male is only 2 inches long; half of its length is taken up by its bill and tail.

Smallest mammal
The rare Kitti's hog-nosed bat is the smallest land mammal. It has a wingspan of less than 5 inches and weighs no more than 0.07 ounce.

Slow mover
The three-toed sloth moves along the ground at speeds of only about 6 feet a minute. In the trees it is a little faster – reaching a top speed of about 10 feet a minute.

Biggest bird
The ostrich is the largest bird in the world. Males can be up to 9 feet tall and weigh 350 pounds. Ostriches are also the fastest two-legged animals, running at speeds of up to 45 mph.

Longest wings
The wandering albatross has the largest wingspan of any living bird. Its wings can measure over 11 feet 6 inches from one tip to the other. This albatross sometimes flies more than 500 miles in a day.

Long tail
The male quetzal has huge tail feathers that are more than twice the length of his body. He uses them to attract a mate and sheds them after the breeding season.

Egg-beater
The ocean sunfish lays more eggs than any other fish. One female was found to be carrying 300 million eggs.

Long tongue
The chameleon can extend its tongue to almost twice the length of its body. It shoots out its tongue with lightning speed and traps insects on the sticky tip.

Big mouth
The egg-eating snake can swallow eggs twice the size of its own head. Its jaws are hinged with special ligaments that stretch open to allow the egg to pass down its throat.

Short life
The adult mayfly lives for only a few days. It spends its short life looking for a mate. Its young may live for a year or more.

Deadly poison
The king cobra from southeastern Asia is the longest poisonous snake in the world. It can reach a length of over 14 feet.

Fiercest fish
Piranhas are the most ferocious freshwater fish in the world. They will attack any creature in the water, no matter how big it is, and have been known to kill people and horses.

Living mouthful
The banded yellow mouthbrooder protects her young by holding them in her mouth while they are small. She spits out the young fish so that they can feed.

Long life
Tuataras often live for 120 years or more. The eggs may take up to 15 months to hatch.

Rare mammal
The thylacine was hunted almost to extinction, and the last animal was thought to have died in a zoo in the 1930s. But there were reported sightings of thylacines in remote parts of Tasmania in the 1970s and 1980s.

Egg-laying mammal
The platypus is an unusual mammal because it lays eggs. When the young hatch out, they feed on their mother's milk, which they suck off the fur on her stomach.

Mate-eater
The female black widow spider often eats the male spider after he has mated with her. She contains poison that is 15 times more powerful than the poison of a rattlesnake.

Talking birds
Pet parrots can be taught to use words to tell their trainers what they want. They can also learn to choose the right colors, shapes, and numbers.

Longest journey
Every year, the Arctic tern migrates from the Arctic to the Antarctic and back, a round trip of 16,000 miles.

Smelly spray
The skunk sprays a nasty-smelling liquid over its enemies and can hit a target accurately from about 12 feet away.

Noisiest animal
The howler monkeys of the Central American rainforests are the noisiest land animals. Their calls can be heard up to 3 miles away.

Animals in danger

SINCE LIFE BEGAN ON EARTH about 3.5 billion years ago, as many as 500 million species of plants and animals may have lived on our planet. Over millions of years, some of these plants and animals died out because of changes in the environment. New species developed that were better suited to the changed conditions, and they replaced the older species. This slow process of change is called evolution. Some species survive for tens of millions of years without evolving much at all. Others die out after only a few thousand years.

Nowadays, species are becoming extinct much faster than they would naturally because of things that people do, such as hunting animals and destroying habitats. This is likely to upset the delicate balance of life on the planet. You can find out more about things that threaten animals by reading across the bottom of these two pages. Three-quarters of the extinctions that happened in the last 300 years were caused by people. At the moment, scientists think that thousands of species of plants and animals are endangered and may become extinct by the year 2000. This includes 1,000 species of birds and over 500 mammals. All of the species shown on this map have drastically declined in numbers, and some are near extinction.

Imagine a world without elephants, rhinos, and giant pandas. It would be tragic if they vanished forever. Animals make our world a more beautiful and interesting place to live. They are also very useful to people. We depend on some animals for food and medicine, and to help us grow crops and carry heavy things. There are many ways in which we can help to protect endangered animals. You can read about some of them on the next page.

HABITAT DESTRUCTION

The main threat to the survival of endangered animals comes from people destroying their habitat. Each species of animal is suited to its particular surroundings and usually cannot move elsewhere if this habitat is destroyed. Forests are often cut down to harvest timber or to make way for farms, mines, roads, and cities, endangering animals such as the Spanish lynx or gorilla that once lived there. Once the trees are removed, the soil may be washed away by the rain or blown away by the wind, creating land which is of no use to people or animals. Marshlands and swamps are drained to provide more space for the rapidly increasing human population. Hedges are dug up to make huge fields where farm machines can work more easily. Land may also be flooded to make reservoirs that supply cities with water or to produce electricity inside large dams.

In some countries, large areas of countryside have been destroyed to extract minerals or fuel from under the ground.

HUNTING AND COLLECTING

Many animals are hunted for sport or for valuable parts of their bodies. Animals with beautiful skins, such as leopards, cheetahs, ocelots, and caimans, are killed so that their skins can be made into coats, shoes, or bags. Most of this killing is illegal, but as long as people are willing to pay for the goods, the trade will go on. Often animals are killed for one part of their body, such as the horns or tusks, and the rest of the body is left to rot. Rhinos, for example, are killed for their horns, which are used to make dagger handles and Chinese folk medicines.

In the past, many animals were taken from the wild to become part of scientific collections. Nowadays, scientists are more interested in preserving wild animals in their natural habitats. But some wild animals are still collected for medical research or for sale as pets. Rare butterflies, such as the blue morpho, are endangered by butterfly collectors, while many rare birds are put at greater risk of extinction by people who steal their eggs for collections.

Blue morpho butterfly

Spanish lynx

Since 1945, over half the rainforest in the world have been destroyed. Every minute, an area of rainforest the size of 50 football fields is destroyed. At this rate, all the rainforests could disappear within the next 50 years.

Many ocelots have been killed for their spotted coats, and the species is now very rare. The rats they used to eat have increased in numbers and spread diseases to people.

Fur coats are a luxury. We can survive without them, and we can even make artificial fur coats that look just like the real thing. These fur coats would look much better if left on the animals they came from.

There are probably only about 300 mountain gorillas left in central Africa. They are threatened mainly by the destruction of their forest habitat, but if they were preserved as a tourist attraction, they could draw badly needed money to the area.

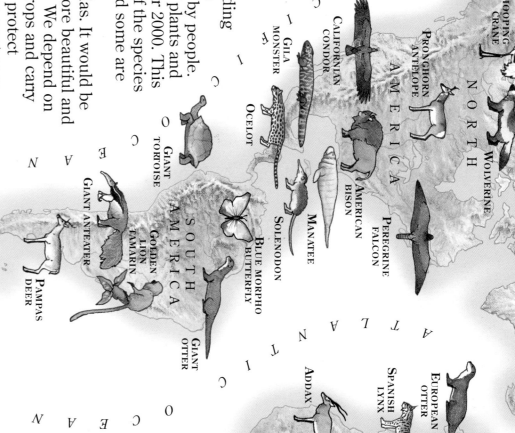

WHOOPING CRANE

PRONGHORN ANTELOPE

WOLVERINE

GILA MONSTER

CALIFORNIAN CONDOR

NORTH AMERICA

PEREGRINE FALCON

OCELOT

AMERICAN BISON

MANATEE

GIANT TORTOISE

SOLENODON

BLUE MORPHO BUTTERFLY

GIANT ANTEATER

GOLDEN LION TAMARIN

SOUTH AMERICA

GIANT OTTER

PAMPAS DEER

PACIFIC OCEAN

ATLANTIC OCEAN

ADDAX

SPANISH LYNX

EUROPEAN OTTER

WHAT WE CAN DO TO HELP

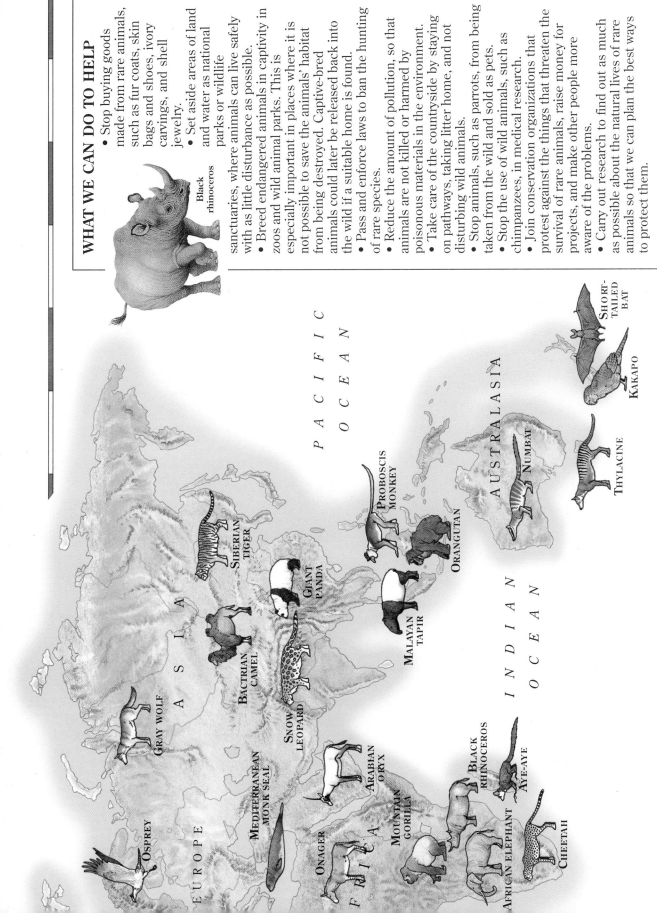

- Stop buying goods made from rare animals, such as fur coats, skin bags and shoes, ivory carvings, and shell jewelry.
- Set aside areas of land and water as national parks or wildlife sanctuaries, where animals can live safely with as little disturbance as possible.
- Breed endangered animals in captivity in zoos and wild animal parks. This is especially important in places where it is not possible to save the animals' habitat from being destroyed. Captive-bred animals could later be released back into the wild if a suitable home is found.
- Pass and enforce laws to ban the hunting of rare species.
- Reduce the amount of pollution, so that animals are not killed or harmed by poisonous materials in the environment.
- Take care of the countryside by staying on pathways, taking litter home, and not disturbing wild animals.
- Stop animals, such as parrots, from being taken from the wild and sold as pets.
- Stop the use of wild animals, such as chimpanzees, in medical research.
- Join conservation organizations that protest against the things that threaten the survival of rare animals, raise money for projects, and make other people more aware of the problems.
- Carry out research to find out as much as possible about the natural lives of rare animals so that we can plan the best ways to protect them.

Black rhinoceros

OSPREY
GRAY WOLF
SIBERIAN TIGER
BACTRIAN CAMEL
GIANT PANDA
MEDITERRANEAN MONK SEAL
SNOW LEOPARD
ARABIAN ORYX
ONAGER
MALAYAN TAPIR
MOUNTAIN GORILLA
BLACK RHINOCEROS
AYE-AYE
AFRICAN ELEPHANT
CHEETAH
PROBOSCIS MONKEY
ORANGUTAN
NUMBAT
SHORT-TAILED BAT
KAKAPO
THYLACINE

E U R O P E
A S I A
A F R I C A
A U S T R A L A S I A
P A C I F I C   O C E A N
I N D I A N   O C E A N

INTRODUCED SPECIES

Galápagos giant tortoise

People take animals from one country to another. Some of these introduced species are not suited to their new home and die out. Others flourish and increase in numbers, upsetting the balance of life among animals already living in the country. On the Galápagos Islands, for instance, introduced goats compete with the native giant tortoises and land iguanas for food, while introduced rats and wild cats eat the eggs and young of tortoises and birds. Flightless birds in New Zealand, such as the kakapo, are endangered because introduced cats, rats, stoats, and ferrets eat their eggs and young.

Some species are introduced to a country to solve one problem but end up causing much more serious problems. Cane toads were introduced to Australia to eat beetles that were destroying the sugar cane crop. These poisonous toads spread fast because there were no natural enemies in Australia to control their numbers. They now threaten the survival of native frogs, reptiles, and small mammals.

Large herds of pampas deer once grazed on the pampas, but competition from farm animals has drastically reduced their numbers.

Farmers have introduced large herds of grazing animals, such as sheep and cattle, to the grassy plains of the pampas in South America. This has changed the landscape, as farmers often start fires to encourage the growth of new grass for cattle to eat.

POLLUTION

Many farmers use chemicals to help them grow bigger crops and fight pests and diseases. But these chemicals seep into the soil and rivers and may poison wildlife. Poisonous chemicals from factories and sewage works may also be dumped into rivers or the sea. Another form of pollution, acid rain, is caused when the chemicals from vehicle exhausts, power stations, and factories combine with water in the air and fall as rain. Rainwater collects in streams and rivers and flows into lakes, making their waters more acidic and killing the fish that live in them. Birds such as ospreys eat the fish and suffer because the poisons become concentrated in their bodies. They may lay eggs with thin shells and have chicks with deformed bones. Acid rain also destroys forests, particularly conifer trees with needle-like leaves, reducing the habitats available for animals.

A particularly dangerous form of pollution is radioactivity. In 1986, an accident at the Chernobyl nuclear power station in the Ukraine released high levels of radiation into the air and it drifted over much of Europe. The effects of this radiation on wildlife are still being investigated.

Osprey

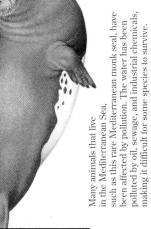

Many animals that live in the Mediterranean Sea, such as this rare Mediterranean monk seal, have been affected by pollution. The water has been polluted by oil, sewage, and industrial chemicals, making it difficult for some species to survive.

Oil sometimes escapes into the sea after a tanker runs aground or hits another ship. Oil makes birds' feathers stick together, so that they cannot keep out the cold and wet. The birds are unable to dive for food. They eventually die from cold and hunger.

Index

Acknowledgments

Dorling Kindersley would like to thank the following: Rachel Foster and David Gillingwater for additional design help, Struan Reid for editorial assistance, and Lynn Bresler for compiling the index.

Picture research Cynthia Hole

Maps Aziz Khan

Picture Credits
A=above, B=below, C=centre, L=left, R=right, T=top

Bryan and Cherry Alexander Photographers: 9T; 9BL; 9BR; 59T
Heather Angel: 7C; 51C
Ardea: 49CR
J.Allan Cash Photolibrary: 5BR; 5BL; 5CR; 6TR; 6TC; 23T; 33TL; 46L; 49BL; 51T; 54T; 62L
Bruce Coleman Ltd: 16; 37BL; 41B; 47
Richard Czapnik: 34BR
Dorling Kindersley/Dave King: 5TR
Chris Fairclough Colour Library: 10T; 11; 13C; 13R; 15; 18; 30; 31TL; 31BR; 32; 34TL; 35; 39T; 39C; 39B; 52T; 52B; 53; 54C; 54B; 57TL; 58BL; 58C; 58TR; 59CR
Geoscience Features Picture Library: 5CL; 20BL; 29BR; 46R
Robert Harding Picture Library: 5TL; 7CL; 7T; 7CR; 7BL; 37T; 41T; 45T; 45BL; 51B
Hutchison Library: 13L; 15TL; 17; 27BL; 37BR; 45CR; 49T
Image Bank: 6TL; 7BR; 15B; 17B; 19T; 19B; 29T; 29CL; 33BR; 56CR; 59BL
Peter Johnson/NHPA: 41C
John Massey Stewart: 42R
Tony Morrison/South American Pictures: 6B; 23B; 23C; 27T
Papilio: 20TC; 20TR; 24; 25L; 25R
Photographers Library: 57BR
Power Pix: 56TL; 56BL
Rex Features: 62R
Travel Photo International: 10B; 27BR; 42L; 63L
Rose Winall/ICCE: 63R